821/MAT

SHOUT
WHISPER
& SING

SHOUT WHISPER & SING

101 POEMS TO READ ALOUD

Compiled by Beverley Mathias

Illustrated by Victor Ambrus

The Bodley Head
London

First published in the UK by The Bodley Head, 1989
Conceived, designed and produced by Signpost Books, Ltd.
44 Uxbridge Street, London W8 7TG
Copyright in this format © 1989 Signpost Books Ltd.
This collection copyright © 1989 Beverley Mathias
Illustrations copyright © 1989 Victor Ambrus
Compiler: Beverley Mathias
Designer: Ned Hoste
Editor: Felicity Trotman

British Library Cataloguing in Publication Data
Shout whisper and sing
I. Mathias, Beverley
II. Ambrus, Victor
821'.914'0809282

ISBN 0–370–31383–6

Typeset by DP Photosetting, Aylesbury, Bucks
Printed in Great Britain for
The Bodley Head Ltd
32 Bedford Square, London WC1B 3SG
by the Bath Press, Avon

First published 1989

Contents

3 For Visiting Relatives and Other Family Occasions

4 For Sharing With Friends

Dedicated to my parents who introduced me to poetry

Introduction

During a period of your life, usually between the ages of six and fourteen years, you will be asked to recite a poem. Often it is because you look cute – no front teeth, lanky and long-legged, lovely curly hair, new glasses – but frequently it is because your parents are proud of you and want other members of the family to know how clever you are.

You don't want to recite poetry, but you can't refuse without being sent to bed, refused supper, made to feel unhelpful, told it's a stage you're going through, or accused of being plain mutinous.

Grandma likes nice poems, Auntie likes weepy ones, Grandad and Uncle prefer something with a bit of guts, Mum and Dad like them short, the cousins prefer gore or a giggle. So you search and decide to give them something nobody wants – a long poem. Your relatives sit … and sit … and sit …

This collection is for you, and for your adult friends who can remember being a child. It is also for fun. Some of the poetry is so tense as to be funny when read today, other poems are sad, there are some which are genuinely funny, and others which take a great deal of effort to read, let alone learn. They come from all over the English-speaking world. Some are about battles now forgotten, or at least faded into time, others are about events which no one can now recall.

Poetry is for reading, and for sharing some of the time, and a lot of it needs to be shouted aloud in order to be enjoyed. Other poems are for quieter moments. Poetry tells a story, explains a situation, gives vent to feelings, but above all it is a celebration of language.

There are one-hundred-and-one poems in this collection because it's always the one you haven't got that is the one you need, so one hundred didn't seem to be enough. Most of the poets are dead, but the language they use is not. Some of the dialects might be strange, but slang doesn't change all that much.

No doubt everyone reading this collection will wonder why some particular favourite of theirs has been omitted. Having started off collecting poems it became hard to stop. People kept asking for their favourite to be included and the line had to be drawn somewhere. There are poems which can be dramatised by the dramatic, told in tones of doom by those so inclined, and others which just seem to trip off the tongue. Very few of these poems were actually written for children.

Anyway, for what it's worth, here they are. I enjoyed finding and rereading them, I hope you enjoy discovering and rediscovering them – then introducing them to your relatives and friends.

Beverley Mathias
March 1989

To be Whispered While Waiting at Airports and Stations

Abou Ben Adhem   LEIGH HUNT

This short humorous moral tale tells how a man can give the right answers for the wrong reasons and still receive his reward.

Abou Ben Adhem (may his tribe increase!)
Awoke one night from a deep dream of peace,
And saw, within the moonlight in his room,
Making it rich, and like a lily in bloom,
An angel writing in a book of gold: –
Exceeding peace had made Ben Adhem bold,
And to the presence in the room he said,
    "What writest thou?" – The vision rais'd its head,
And with a look made of all sweet accord,
Answer'd, "The names of those who love the Lord."
    "And is mine one?" said Abou. "Nay, not so,"
Replied the angel. Abou spoke more low,
But cheerly still; and said, "I pray thee, then,
Write me as one that loves his fellow men."
    The angel wrote, and vanish'd. The next night
It came again with a great wakening light,
And show'd the names whom love of God had blest,
And lo! Ben Adhem's name led all the rest.

The Arrow and the Song

HENRY WADSWORTH LONGFELLOW

*The first two lines are well-known, the rest is quick to learn
and makes an ideal filler-in-of-time, especially if you imagine
the arrow and where you might have sent it. Perhaps to the
friends you are meeting.*

I shot an arrow into the air,
It fell to earth, I knew not where;
For, so swiftly it flew, the sight
Could not follow it in its flight.

I breathed a song into the air,
It fell to earth, I knew not where;
For who has sight so keen and strong
That it can follow the flight of song?

Long, long afterward, in an oak
I found the arrow, still unbroke;
And the song, from beginning to end,
I found again in the heart of a friend.

Cargoes

JOHN MASEFIELD

*For me this has always conjured up pictures of faraway places
and graceful sailing ships. Waiting for Concorde might be a
good time to recite this to yourself, after all, it is a modern-day
"ship" of the skies.*

Quinquireme of Nineveh from distant Ophir
Rowing home to haven in sunny Palestine,
With a cargo of ivory,
And apes and peacocks,
Sandalwood, cedarwood, and sweet white wine.

Stately Spanish galleon coming from the Isthmus,
Dipping through the Tropics by the palm-green shores,
With a cargo of diamonds,
Emeralds, amethysts,
Topazes, and cinnamon, and gold moidores.

Dirty British coaster with a salt-caked smoke-stack
Butting through the Channel in the mad March days,
With a cargo of Tyne coal,
Road-rails, pig-lead,
Firewood, iron-ware, and cheap tin trays.

Daffodils

WILLIAM WORDSWORTH

*There is nothing more boring than waiting for a plane or train
which is late. This poem brings to mind days of sunshine and
fresh breezes so that you can imagine yourself where you first
saw "a host of golden daffodils". I first saw mine in New
Zealand, while working in Dunedin many years ago.*

I wander'd lonely as a cloud
   That floats on high o'er vales and hills,
When all at once I saw a crowd,
   A host, of golden daffodils;
Beside the lake, beneath the trees,
Fluttering and dancing in the breeze.

Continuous as the stars that shine
   And twinkle on the Milky Way,
They stretch'd in never-ending line
   Along the margin of a bay:
Ten thousand saw I at a glance,
Tossing their heads in sprightly dance.

The waves beside them danced, but they
   Out-did the sparkling waves in glee:
A poet could not but be gay,
   In such a jocund company:
I gazed – and gazed – but little thought
What wealth the show to me had brought:

For oft, when on my couch I lie
   In vacant or in pensive mood,
They flash upon that inward eye
   Which is the bliss of solitude;
And then my heart with pleasure fills,
And dances with the daffodils.

I Remember, I Remember

THOMAS HOOD

Childhood is a time we want to leave, and later remember with
affection. Waiting is a good time for remembering as you can
clear your mind and concentrate on events of the past, while
waiting for the friend who shared your childhood.

I remember, I remember
The house where I was born,
The little window where the sun
Came peeping in at morn;
He never came a wink too soon
Nor brought too long a day;
But now, I often wish the night
Had borne my breath away.

I remember, I remember
The roses, red and white,
The violets, and the lily-cups –
Those flowers made of light!
The lilacs where the robin built,
And where my brother set
The laburnum on his birthday, –
The tree is living yet!

I remember, I remember
Where I was used to swing,
And thought the air must rush as fresh
To swallows on the wing;
My spirit flew in feathers then
That is so heavy now,
The summer pools could hardly cool
The fever on my brow.

I remember, I remember
The fir-trees dark and high;
I used to think their slender tops
Were close against the sky:
It was a childish ignorance,
But now 'tis little joy
To know I'm farther off from Heaven
Than when I was a boy.

If

RUDYARD KIPLING

*Dreaming of fame and fortune is part of growing, and
dreaming is part of waiting too. So here's one to impress
people while you are waiting, especially if the person you are
waiting for is someone whose judgement you respect and value,
as this poem is about self-confidence and humility. Don't be
misled by the last line: "man" means woman too!*

If you can keep your head when all about you
    Are losing theirs and blaming it on you;
If you can trust yourself when all men doubt you,
    But make allowance for their doubting too;
If you can wait and not be tired by waiting,
    Or being lied about, don't deal in lies,
Or being hated don't give way to hating,
    And yet don't look too good, nor talk too wise;
If you can dream – and not make dreams your master;
    If you can think – and not make thoughts your aim;
If you can meet with Triumph and Disaster
    And treat those two imposters just the same;
If you can bear to hear the truth you've spoken
    Twisted by knaves to make a trap for fools,
    Or watch the things you gave your life to broken,
    And stoop and build 'em up with worn-out tools;
If you can make one heap of all your winnings
    And risk it in one turn of pitch-and-toss,
And lose, and start again at your beginnings,
    And never breathe a word about your loss;
If you can force your heart and nerve and sinew
    To serve your turn long after they are gone,
And so hold on when there is nothing in you
    Except the Will which says to them:"Hold on!"
If you can talk with crowds and keep your virtue,
    Or walk with Kings – nor lose the common touch;
If neither foes nor loving friends can hurt you;
    If all men count with you, but none too much;
    If you can fill the unforgiving minute
    With sixty seconds' worth of distance run;
Yours is the Earth and everything that's in it,
    And – which is more – you'll be a Man, my son!

Old Meg

JOHN KEATS

*Do you ever find yourself watching the waiting crowd and
wondering who they are and why they are in that place at that
time? Perhaps you might see Old Meg in the crowd, out of
place in her cloak and hat, yet at one with her environment.
Amidst the clatter and bustle of a busy waiting-place, it might
help to remember the tranquillity of Old Meg's life.*

Old Meg she was a Gipsey,
    And liv'd upon the Moors;
Her bed it was the brown heath turf,
    And her house was out of doors.

Her apples were swart blackberries,
    Her currants, pods o'broom;
Her wine was dew of the wild white rose,
    Her book a churchyard tomb.

Her Brothers were the craggy hills,
    Her Sisters larchen trees;
Alone with her great family
    She liv'd as she did please.

No breakfast had she many a morn,
    No dinner many a noon,
And, 'stead of supper, she would stare
    Full hard against the moon.

But every morn, of woodbine fresh
    She made her garlanding,
And, every night, the dark glen Yew
    She wove, and she would sing.

And with her fingers, old and brown,
    She plaited Mats o' Rushes,
And gave them to the cottagers
    She met among the Bushes.

Old Meg was brave as Margaret Queen
    And tall as Amazon;
An old red blanket cloak she wore,
    A chip hat had she on.
God rest her aged bones somewhere!
    She died full long agone!

Robin

IAIN CRICHTON SMITH

*Out of the windows of trains waiting in stations, buses waiting
at stops, you often see birds about their daily business. This
poem is short and could easily be brought to mind as you watch
a robin foraging along the path for his breakfast.*

If on a frosty morning
the robin redbreast calls
his waistcoat red and burning
like a beggar at your walls

throw bread crumbs on the grass for him
when the ground is hard and still
for in his breast there is a flame
that winter cannot kill.

The Sands of Dee CHARLES KINGSLEY

Another mind picture to rid your sight of seething masses of people. The still calmness of an isolated beach, a girl calling cattle, and the cruel sea taking her as she walked through the mist. Not a happy poem.

O Mary, go and call the cattle home,
  And call the cattle home,
  And call the cattle home,
 Across the sands of Dee.
The western wind was wild and dank with foam,
 And all alone went she.

The western tide crept up along the sand,
  And o'er and o'er the sand,
  And round and round the sand,
 As far as eye could see.
The rolling mist came down and hid the land;
 And never home came she.

"Oh! is it weed, or fish, or floating hair –
  A tress of golden hair,
  A drownèd maiden's hair,
 Above the nets at sea?"
Was never salmon yet that shone so fair
 Among the stakes of Dee.

They rowed her in across the rolling foam,
  The cruel, crawling foam,
  The cruel, hungry foam,
 To her grave beside the sea.
But still the boatmen hear her call the cattle home
 Across the sands of Dee.

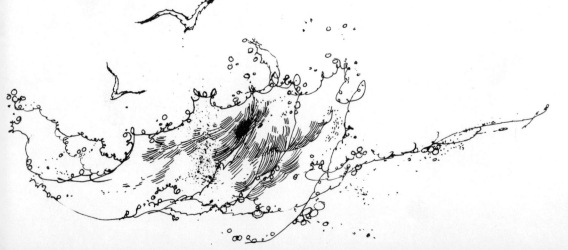

Sea-Fever

JOHN MASEFIELD

*This is best when waiting for ships; even the cross-channel
ferry will do. I used to live by the sea, and spent my childhood
watching ships coming and going from the harbour, wondering
where they had been and where they were going. I still miss
being able to "go down to the sea" to watch the ships come in.*

I must go down to the seas again, to the lonely sea and the sky,
And all I ask is a tall ship and a star to steer her by,
And the wheel's kick and the wind's song and the white sail's
    shaking,
And a grey mist on the sea's face and a grey dawn breaking.

I must go down to the seas again, for the call of the running tide
Is a wild call and a clear call that may not be denied;
And all I ask is a windy day with the white clouds flying,
And the flung spray and the blown spume, and the sea-gulls
    crying.

I must go down to the seas again, to the vagrant gypsy life,
To the gull's way and the whale's way where the wind's like a
    whetted knife;
And all I ask is a merry yarn from a laughing fellow-rover,
And quiet sleep and a sweet dream when the long trick's over.

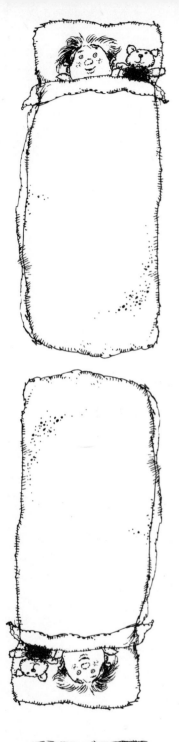

The Sleeping-bag

HERBERT GEORGE PONTING

I hate sleeping-bags! The outside is always cold and the inside always wraps itself round me so that I feel I am in a permanent spiral. This poem is a good one for learning so that you can recite it to yourself when you are bored stiff with waiting. It's bound to make you laugh, but remember you must concentrate very hard to get it right and not end up with your insides upside down.

On the outside grows the furside, on the inside grows the skin-
    side;
So the furside is the outside, and the skinside is the inside.
As the skinside is the inside, and the furside is the outside;
One "side" likes the skinside inside, and the furside on the
    outside.
Others like the skinside outside, and the furside on the inside;
As the skinside is the hardside, and the furside is the soft side.
If you turn the skinside outside, thinking you will side with that
    "side",
Then the soft side, furside's inside, which some argue is the
    wrong side.
If you turn the furside outside, as you say it grows on that side;
Then your outside's next the skinside, which for comfort's not
    the right side:
For the skinside is the cold side, and your outside's not your
    warm side;
And two cold sides coming side by side are not right sides one
    "side" decides.
If you decide to side with that "side," turn the outside, furside,
    inside;
Then the hard side, cold side, skinside's, beyond all question,
    inside outside.

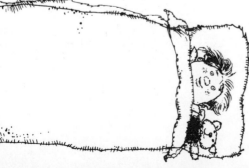

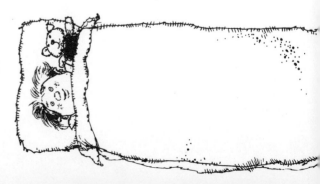

Tarantella

HILAIRE BELLOC

On the way to Spain, Portugal, South America or Mexico might be a good time to remember this poem. I wonder who Miranda was?

Do you remember an Inn, Miranda?
Do you remember an Inn?
And the tedding and the spreading
Of the straw for a bedding,
And the fleas that tease in the High Pyrenees,
And the wine that tasted of the tar,
And the cheers and the jeers of the young muleteers
(Under the vine of the dark verandah)?
Do you remember an Inn, Miranda,
Do you remember an Inn?
And the cheers and the jeers of the young muleteers
Who hadn't got a penny,
And who weren't paying any,
And the hammer at the doors and the Din?
And the Hip! Hop! Hap!
Of the clap
Of the hands to the twirl and the swirl
Of the girl gone chancing,
Glancing,
Dancing,
Backing and advancing,
Snapping of the clapper to the spin
Out and in –
And the Ting, Tong, Tang of the Guitar!
Do you remember an Inn,
Miranda?
Do you remember an Inn?
Never more;
Miranda,
Never more.
Only the high peaks hoar:
And Aragon a torrent at the door.
No sound
In the walls of the Halls where falls
The tread
Of the feet of the dead to the ground.
No sound:
But the boom
Of the far Waterfall like Doom.

The Tiger WILLIAM BLAKE

*This is probably one of Blake's best known poems. It can help
alleviate the boredom of waiting if you look at the station or
airport as a potential jungle with all sorts of wild beasts lurking
behind counters and trolleys. You can "see" the tiger and
admire him as Blake does without fear of being discovered.*

Tiger, tiger, burning bright
In the forests of the night!
What immortal hand or eye
Could frame thy fearful symmetry?

In what distant deeps or skies
Burnt the ardour of thine eyes?
On what wings dare he aspire –
What the hand dare seize the fire?

And what shoulder and what art
Could twist the sinews of thy heart?
And when thy heart began to beat,
What dread hand formed thy dread feet?

What the hammer, what the chain,
In what furnace was thy brain?
Did God smile his work to see?
Did He who made the lamb make thee?

Woodman, Spare That Tree

GEORGE P. MORRIS

*Trees are friends, and although there are very few in waiting-
places, you could imagine the pillars and posts as trees and
decide which ones you would not want to see cut down. I
remember with sadness a lovely old pine tree I used to climb,
long after I was supposedly grown up, which was unfortunately
burnt in a fire. I wish that tree had been spared.*

Woodman, spare that tree! Touch not a single bough!
In youth it sheltered me, and I'll protect it now.
'Twas my forefather's hand that placed it near his cot;
There, woodman, let it stand; thy axe shall harm it not!

That old familiar tree, whose glory and renown
Are spread o'er land and sea. And wouldst thou hew it down?
Woodman, forbear thy stroke! Cut not its earth-bound ties;
O, spare that aged oak, now towering to the skies.

When but an idle boy I sought its grateful shade;
In all their gushing joy here, too, my sisters played.
My mother kissed me here, my father pressed my hand;
Forgive the foolish tear; but let that old oak stand.

My heart-strings round thee cling, close as thy bark, old friend;
Here shall the wild bird sing, and still thy branches bend.
Old tree, the storm still brave! And, woodman, leave the spot;
While I've a hand to save, thy axe shall harm it not.

To Shout Aloud When Walking

Barbara Frietchie

JOHN GREENLEAF WHITTIER

This is the very first poem I ever learnt for myself. I was seven and fell in love with the wonderful drama of the story. It's a very good poem for shouting especially the middle third where Stonewall Jackson rides in leading his men. A vigorous walk is a good time for this one.

Up from the meadows rich with corn,
Clear in the cool September morn,

The clustered spires of Frederick stand
Green-walled by the hills of Maryland.

Round about them orchards sweep,
Apple and peach tree fruited deep,

Fair as the garden of the Lord
To the eyes of the famished rebel horde,

On that pleasant morn of the early fall
When Lee marched over the mountain wall;

Over the mountains winding down,
Horse and foot, into Frederick town.

Forty flags with their silver stars,
Forty flags with their crimson bars,

Flapped in the morning wind: the sun
Of noon looked down, and saw not one.

Up rose old Barbara Frietchie then,
Bowed with her fourscore years and ten;

Bravest of all in Frederick town,
She took up the flag the men hauled down;

In her attic window the staff she set,
To show that one heart was loyal yet.

Up the street came the rebel tread,
Stonewall Jackson riding ahead.

Under his slouched hat left and right
He glanced; the old flag met his sight.

"Halt!" – the dust-brown ranks stood fast,
"Fire!" – out blazed the rifle-blast.

It shivered the window, pane and sash;
It rent the banner with seam and gash.

Quick as it fell, from the broken staff
Dame Barbara snatched the silken scarf.

She leaned far out on the window-sill,
And shook it forth with a royal will.

"Shoot, if you must, this old gray head,
But spare your country's flag," she said.

A shade of sadness, a blush of shame,
Over the face of the leader came;

The nobler nature within him stirred
To life at that woman's deed and word;

"Who touches a hair of yon gray head
Dies like a dog! March on!" he said.

All day long through Frederick street
Sounded the tread of marching feet:

All day long that free flag tossed
Over the heads of the rebel host.

Ever its torn folds rose and fell
On the loyal winds that loved it well;

And through the hill-gaps sunset light
Shone over it with a warm good-night.

Barbara Frietchie's work is o'er,
And the Rebel rides on his raids no more.

Honour to her! and let a tear
Fall, for her sake, on Stonewall's bier.

Over Barbara Frietchie's grave,
Flag of Freedom and Union, wave!

Peace and order and beauty draw
Round thy symbol of light and law;

And ever the stars above look down
On the stars below in Frederick town!

Casabianca

FELICIA HEMANS

*You need to be feeling dramatic for this. It's best said with
great feeling and elaborate gestures somewhere where nobody
is going to hear, because then you can imagine the sea raging
and roaring while you stand on a seat in the park and try to
hear the command to abandon ship.*

The boy stood on the burning deck
    Whence all but he had fled;
The flame that lit the battle's wreck
    Shone round him o'er the dead.

The flames rolled on. He would not go
    Without his father's word;
That father faint in death below,
    His voice no longer heard.

He called aloud: "Say, father, say
    If yet my task is done!"
He knew not that the chieftain lay
    Unconscious of his son.

"Speak, father!" once again he cried,
    "If I may yet be gone!"
And but the booming shots replied,
    And fast the flames rolled on.

Upon his brow he felt their breath,
    And in his waving hair,
And looked from that lone post of death
    In still yet brave despair;

And shouted but once more aloud,
    "My father! must I stay?"
While o'er him fast through sail and shroud,
    The wreathing fires made way.

They wrapt the ship in splendour wild,
    They caught the flag on high,
And streamed above the gallant child
    Like banners in the sky.

Then came a burst of thunder-sound –
    The boy – oh! where was he?
Ask of the winds that far around
    With fragments strewed the sea,

With mast, and helm and pennon fair,
    That well had borne their part.
But the noblest thing that perished there
    Was that young faithful heart.

Casey at the Bat

ERNEST LAWRENCE THAYER

*Growing up in a home where baseball was the chief sport, this
poem brings back all manner of memories of games lost and
won on the third strike in the last inning of the game. In
baseball a player can be struck out by missing three hits, can
walk to first base if the pitcher sends down four balls out of the
strike zone, or he can be covered in glory, as Casey usually was,
by hitting the ball into the outfield. Imagine the horror when
the best hitter hears "strike three – you're out!"*

The outlook wasn't brilliant for the Mudville nine that day:
The score stood four to two with but one inning more to play.
And then when Cooney died at first, and Barrows did the same,
A sickly silence fell upon the patrons of the game.

A straggling few got up to go in deep despair. The rest
Clung to that hope which springs eternal in the human breast;
They thought if only Casey could but get a whack at that –
We'd put up even money now with Casey at the bat.

But Flynn preceded Casey, as did also Jimmy Blake,
And the former was a lulu and the latter was a cake;
So upon that stricken multitude grim melancholy sat,
For there seemed but little chance of Casey's getting to the bat.

But Flynn let drive a single, to the wonderment of all,
And Blake, the much despised, tore the cover off the ball;
And when the dust had lifted, and the men saw what had
    occurred,
There was Jimmy safe at second and Flynn a-hugging third.

Then from 5,000 throats and more there rose a lusty yell;
It rumbled through the valley, it rattled in the dell;
It knocked upon the mountain and recoiled upon the flat,
For Casey, mighty Casey, was advancing to the bat.

There was ease in Casey's manner as he stepped into his place;
There was pride in Casey's bearing and a smile on Casey's face.
And when, responding to the cheers, he lightly doffed his hat,
No stranger in the crowd could doubt 'twas Casey at the bat.

Ten thousand eyes were on him as he rubbed his hands with dirt;
Five thousand tongues applauded when he wiped them on his
     shirt.
Then while the writhing pitcher ground the ball into his hip,
Defiance gleamed in Casey's eye, a sneer curled Casey's lip.

And now the leather-covered sphere came hurtling through the
     air,
And Casey stood a-watching it in haughty grandeur there.
Close by the sturdy batsman the ball unheeded sped –
"That ain't my style," said Casey. "Strike one," the umpire said.

From the benches black with people, there went up a muffled
     roar,
Like the beating of the storm-waves on a stern and distant shore.
"Kill him! Kill the umpire!" shouted some one on the stand;
And it's likely they'd have killed him had not Casey raised his
     hand.

With a smile of Christian charity great Casey's visage shone;
He stilled the rising tumult; he bade the game go on;
He signalled to the pitcher, and once more the spheroid flew;
But Casey still ignored it, and the umpire said, "Strike two."

"Fraud!" cried the maddened thousands, and echo answered
     fraud;
But one scornful look from Casey and the audience was awed.
They saw his face grow stern and cold, they saw his muscles
     strain,
And they knew that Casey wouldn't let that ball go by again.

The sneer is gone from Casey's lip, his teeth are clenched in hate;
He pounds with cruel violence his bat upon the plate.
And now the pitcher holds the ball, and now he lets it go,
And now the air is shattered by the force of Casey's blow.

Oh, somewhere in this favoured land the sun is shining bright;
The band is playing somewhere, and somewhere hearts are light,
And somewhere men are laughing, and somewhere children
     shout;
But there is no joy in Mudville – mighty Casey has struck out.

Casey Jones

T. LAWRENCE SELBERT

*The rhythm of the train is in the words of this poem. The
story is a sad one, but it's ideal for walking along disused
railway tracks as I did recently in Canada. Diesel engines don't
have quite the same magic as steam trains, and Casey is driving
a steam train. I still feel a thrill when a steam whistle blasts out
over the countryside and far off in the distance you see the
puffs of smoke and steam. You'll walk faster and faster as the
words become more urgent with Casey struggling for control.*

Come all you rounders that want to hear
The story of a brave engineer.
Casey Jones was the rounder's name,
On a big eight wheeler, boys, he won his fame.
The caller called Casey at half-past four,
He kissed his wife at the station door,
He mounted to the cabin with the orders in his hand,
And he took his farewell trip to that promis'd land.

Chorus
Casey Jones mounted to his cabin,
Casey Jones with his orders in his hand.
Casey Jones mounted to his cabin,
And he took his farewell trip to that promis'd land.

When he pulled up that Reno hill
He whistled for the crossing with an awful shrill;
The switchman knew by the engine's moan
That the man at the throttle was Casey Jones.
He looked at his water and his water was low;
He looked at his watch and his watch was slow;
He turned to his fireman and this is what he said,
Boy, we're going to reach Frisco, but we'll all be dead.

Chorus
Casey Jones – going to reach Frisco,
Casey Jones – but we'll all be dead,
Casey Jones – going to reach Frisco,
We're going to reach Frisco, but we'll all be dead.

So turn on your water and shovel in your coal,
Stick your head out the window, watch those drivers roll;
I'll drive her till she leaves the rail,
For I'm eight hours late by that Western Mail.
When he was within six miles of the place,
There number four stared him straight in the face.
He turned to his fireman, said, "Jim, you'd better jump,
For there're two locomotives that are going to bump."

Chorus
Casey Jones – two locomotives,
Casey Jones – going to bump,
Casey Jones – two locomotives,
There're two locomotives that are going to bump.

Casey said just before he died,
"There're two more roads I would like to ride."
The fireman said, "Which ones can they be?"
"Oh, the Northern Pacific and the Santa Fe."
Mrs Jones sat at her bed a-sighing
Just to hear the news that her Casey was dying.
"Hush up children, and quit your cryin',
For you've got another poppa on the Salt Lake Line."

Chorus
Casey Jones – got another poppa.
Casey Jones – on the Salt Lake Line,
Casey Jones – got another poppa,
For you've got another poppa on the Salt Lake Line.

The Charge of the Light Brigade

ALFRED, LORD TENNYSON

Most people know the first lines, and probably others as well. It is best shouted aloud with suitable actions, although I would hesitate to say it while on horseback. Some deepseated equine memory might set the horse to defending his country all over again, and you might find yourself in today's equivalent of the charge.

Half a league, half a league,
   Half a league onward,
All in the valley of Death
   Rode the six hundred.
"Forward the Light Brigade!
Charge for the guns!" he said:
Into the valley of Death
   Rode the six hundred.

"Forward the Light Brigade!"
Was there a man dismay'd?
Not tho' the soldier knew
   Some one had blunder'd:
Their's not to make reply,
Their's not to reason why,
Their's but to do and die:
Into the valley of Death
   Rode the six hundred.

Cannon to right of them,
Cannon to left of them,
Cannon in front of them
   Volley'd and thunder'd;
Storm'd at with shot and shell,
Boldly they rode and well,
Into the jaws of Death,
Into the mouth of Hell,
   Rode the six hundred.

Flash'd all their sabres bare,
Flash'd as they turn'd in air,
Sabring the gunners there,
Charging an army, while
   All the world wonder'd:
Plunged in the battery-smoke
Right thro' the line they broke;
Cossack and Russian
Reel'd from the sabre-stroke
   Shatter'd and sunder'd.
Then they rode back, but not,
   Not the six hundred.

Cannon to right of them,
Cannon to left of them,
Cannon behind them
   Volley'd and thunder'd;
Storm'd at with shot and shell,
While horse and hero fell,
They that had fought so well
Came thro' the jaws of Death
Back from the mouth of Hell,
All that was left of them,
   Left of six hundred.

When can their glory fade?
O the wild charge they made!
   All the world wonder'd.
Honour the charge they made!
Honour the Light Brigade,
   Noble six hundred!

The Destruction of Sennacherib

LORD BYRON

*The imagery of this poem effectively recreates an ancient
Hebrew struggle. Saying it aloud on a windswept hillside calls
to mind all the battles which have been fought in the name of
true freedom. A very stirring poem which might leave you
emotionally and physically exhausted.*

The Assyrian came down like a wolf on the fold,
And his cohorts were gleaming in purple and gold;
And the sheen of their spears was like stars on the sea
When the blue wave rolls nightly on deep Galilee.

Like the leaves of the forest when summer is green
That host with their banners at sunset were seen:
Like the leaves of the forest when autumn hath blown
That host on the morrow lay withered and strown!

For the Angel of Death spread his wings on the blast,
And breathed on the face of the foe as he passed;
And the eyes of the sleepers waxed deadly and chill,
And their hearts but once heaved, and for ever grew still!

And there lay the steed with his nostril all wide,
But through it there rolled not the breath of his pride;
And the foam of his gasping lay white on the turf,
And cold as the spray of the rock-beating surf.

And there lay the rider, distorted and pale,
With the dew on his brow and the rust on his mail;
And the tents were all silent, the banners alone,
The lances unlifted, the trumpet unblown.

And the widows of Ashur are loud in their wail,
And the idols are broke in the temple of Baal;
And the might of the Gentile, unsmote by the sword,
Hath melted like snow in the glance of the Lord!

The Fairies

WILLIAM ALLINGHAM

*My father taught me this when I was very small, and he is still
teaching it to his grandchildren. There's something
mesmerizing about the words which even a small child can
recognize. My oldest niece used to call it "the fevver poem". It's
a poem which can shorten a walk and take away the cold
feeling of walking in the rain.*

Up the airy mountain,
    Down the rushy glen,
We daren't go a-hunting
    For fear of little men;
Wee folk, good folk,
    Trooping all together;
Green jacket, red cap,
    And white owl's feather!

Down along the rocky shore
    Some make their home,
They live on crispy pancakes
    Of yellow tide-foam;
Some in the reeds
    Of the black mountain-lake,
With frogs for their watch-dogs,
    All night awake.

High on the hill-top
    The old King sits;
He is now so old and grey
    He's nigh lost his wits.
With a bridge of white mist
    Columbkill he crosses,
On his stately journeys
    From Slieveleague to Rosses;
Or going up with music
    On cold, starry nights,
To sup with the Queen
    Of the gay Northern Lights.

They stole little Bridget
  For seven years long;
When she came down again
  Her friends were all gone.
They took her lightly back,
  Between the night and morrow,
They thought that she was fast asleep,
  But she was dead with sorrow.
They have kept her ever since
  Deep within the lake,
On a bed of flag-leaves,
  Watching till she wake.

By the craggy hill-side,
  Through the mosses bare,
They have planted thorn-trees
  For pleasure here and there.
Is any man so daring
  As dig them up in spite,
He shall find their sharpest thorns
  In his bed at night.

Up the airy mountain,
  Down the rushy glen,
We daren't go a-hunting
  For fear of little men;
Wee folk, good folk,
  Trooping all together;
Green jacket, red cap,
  And white owl's feather!

Hiawatha's Departing

HENRY WADSWORTH LONGFELLOW

Another poem which mesmerizes, but instead of the well-known beginning I have selected the last two stanzas as a lot of readers never reach them, which seems to me to be a pity. The culmination of the epic is also a remembering of all that has gone before. This is for a quiet walk in introspective mood, preferably in forested land with soft leaves and moss underfoot.

By the shore of Gitche Gumee,
By the shining Big-Sea-Water,
At the doorway of his wigwam,
In the pleasant summer morning,
Hiawatha stood and waited.
　　Heavy with the heat and silence
Grew the afternoon of Summer;
With a drowsy sound the forest
Whispered round the sultry wigwam,
With a sound of sleep the water
Rippled on the beach below it;
From the corn-fields shrill and ceaseless
Sang the grasshopper, Pah-puk-keena;
　　Forth into the village went he,
Bade farewell to all the warriors,
Bade farewell to all the young men,
Spake persuading, spake in this wise:
　　"I am going, O my people,
On a long and distant journey;
Many moons and many winters
Will have come, and will have vanished
Ere I come again to see you."
　　On the shore stood Hiawatha,
Turned and waved his hand at parting;
On the clear and luminous water
Launched his birch-canoe for sailing,
From the pebbles of the margin
Shoved it forth into the water;
Whispered to it, "Westward! westward!"
And with speed it darted forward.
　　And the evening sun descending
Set the clouds on fire with redness,
Burned the broad sky, like a prairie,
Left upon the level water

One long track and trail of splendour,
Down whose stream, as down a river,
Westward, westward Hiawatha
Sailed into the fiery sunset,
Sailed into the purple vapours,
Sailed into the dusk of evening.

And the people from the margin
Watched him floating, rising, sinking,
Till the birch-canoe seemed lifted
High into that sea of splendour,
Till it sank into the vapours
Like the new moon slowly, slowly
Sinking in the purple distance.

And they said, "Farewell for ever!"
Said, "Farewell, O Hiawatha!"
And the forests, dark and lonely,
Moved through all their depths of darkness,
Sighed, "Farewell, O Hiawatha!"
And the waves upon the margin
Rising, rippling on the pebbles,
Sobbed, "Farewell, O Hiawatha!"
And the heron, the Shuh-shuh-gah,
From her haunts among the fenlands,
Screamed, "Farewell, O Hiawatha!"

Thus departed Hiawatha,
Hiawatha the Beloved,
In the glory of the sunset,
In the purple mists of evening,
To the regions of the home-wind,
Of the North-west wind Keewaydin,
To the Islands of the Blessed,
To the Kingdom of Ponemah,
To the land of the Hereafter!

Jabberwocky

LEWIS CARROLL

Sheer unadulterated nonsense and well worth learning as it gives new meaning to language. All lovers of Lewis Carroll will know bits of his poems, but this one is wonderful for joyous days out walking with friends, as they probably know the words too, and you can all shout it.

'Twas brillig, and the slithy toves
  Did gyre and gimble in the wabe;
All mimsy were the borogoves,
    And the mome raths outgrabe.

"Beware the Jabberwock, my son!
  The jaws that bite, the claws that catch!
Beware the Jubjub bird, and shun
    The frumious Bandersnatch!"

He took his vorpal sword in hand:
  Long time the manxome foe he sought –
So rested he by the Tumtum tree,
    And stood awhile in thought.

And as in uffish thought he stood,
  The Jabberwock, with eyes of flame,
Came whiffling through the tulgey wood,
    And burbled as it came!

One, two! One, two! And through and through
  The vorpal blade went snicker-snack!
He left it dead, and with its head
    He went galumphing back.

"And hast thou slain the Jabberwock?
  Come to my arms, my beamish boy!
O frabjous day! Callooh! Callay!"
    He chortled in his joy.

'Twas brillig, and the slithy toves
  Did gyre and gimble in the wabe;
All mimsy were the borogoves,
    And the mome raths outgrabe.

Lochinvar

SIR WALTER SCOTT

*A young man strides into a celebration and takes away the
bride, much to the consternation of her friends and relations.
The words are stirring and beg to be said while striding
through the heather. If you have no heather handy a good large
open space will do.*

Oh, young Lochinvar is come out of the West, –
Through all the wide Border his steed was the best,
And save his good broadsword he weapons had none, –
He rode all unarm'd and he rode all alone.
So faithful in love, and so dauntless in war,
There never was knight like the young Lochinvar.

He stay'd not for brake, and he stopp'd not for stone,
He swam the Eske river where ford there was none,
But ere he alighted at Netherby gate,
The bride had consented, the gallant came late;
For a laggard in love and a dastard in war
Was to wed the fair Ellen of brave Lochinvar.

So boldly he enter'd the Netherby hall,
'Mong bridesmen and kinsmen and brothers and all.
Then spoke the bride's father, his hand on his sword
(For the poor craven bridegroom said never a word),
"Oh, come ye in peace here, or come ye in war,
Or to dance at our bridal, young Lord Lochinvar?"

"I long woo'd your daughter, – my suit you denied;
Love swells like the Solway, but ebbs like its tide;
And now am I come, with this lost love of mine
To lead but one measure, drink one cup of wine.
There are maidens in Scotland more lovely, by far,
That would gladly be bride to the young Lochinvar."

The bride kissed the goblet, the knight took it up,
He quaff'd off the wine and he threw down the cup.
She look'd down to blush, and she look'd up to sigh,
With a smile on her lips and a tear in her eye.
He took her soft hand ere her mother could bar:
"Now tread we a measure," said young Lochinvar.

So stately his form, and so lovely her face,
That never a hall such a galliard did grace,
While her mother did fret, and her father did fume,
And the bridegroom stood dangling his bonnet and plume,
And the bridesmaids whisper'd, "Twere better by far
To have match'd our fair cousin with young Lochinvar."

One touch to her hand, and one word in her ear,
When they reach'd the hall-door, and the charger stood near;
So light to the croup the fair lady he swung,
So light to the saddle before her he sprung!
"She is won! we are gone, over bank, bush, and scaur;
They'll have fleet steeds that follow," quoth young Lochinvar.

There was mounting 'mong Graemes of the Netherby clan;
Forsters, Fenwicks, and Musgraves, they rode and they ran;
There was racing and chasing on Cannobie Lee,
But the lost bride of Netherby ne'er did they see.
So daring in love, and so dauntless in war,
Have ye e'er heard of gallant like young Lochinvar?

The Man From Snowy River

A. B. (BANJO) PATERSON

I first heard this recited when I was about nine years old. The person who told the tale was in his eighties, bent with arthritis, but the words riveted me, and this has been a favourite ever since. It smells of eucalyptus forests, and sounds of horses and men. For me it is the epitome of early Australia and simply must be said in the open air.

There was movement at the station, for the word had passed
    around
  That the colt from old Regret had got away,
And had joined the wild bush horses – he was worth a thousand
    pound,
  So all the cracks had gathered to the fray.
All the tried and noted riders from the stations near and far
  Had mustered at the homestead overnight,
For the bushmen love hard riding where the wild bush horses
    are,
  And the stock-horse snuffs the battle with delight.

There was Harrison, who made his pile when Pardon won the
    cup,
  The old man with his hair as white as snow;
But few could ride beside him when his blood was fairly up –
He would go wherever horse and man could go.
And Clancy of the Overflow came down to lend a hand,
  No better horseman ever held the reins;
For never horse could throw him while the saddle-girths would
    stand –
  He learnt to ride while droving on the plains.

And one was there, a stripling on a small and weedy beast;
  He was something like a racehorse undersized,
With a touch of Timor pony – three parts thoroughbred
    at least –
  And such as are by mountain horsemen prized.
He was hard and tough and wiry – just the sort that won't say die –
  There was courage in his quick impatient tread;
And he bore the badge of gameness in his bright and fiery eye,
  And the proud and lofty carriage of his head.

47

But still so slight and weedy, one would doubt his power to stay,
  And the old man said, "That horse will never do
For a long and tiring gallop – lad, you'd better stop away,
  Those hills are far too rough for such as you."
So he waited, sad and wistful – only Clancy stood his friend –
  "I think we ought to let him come," he said;
"I warrant he'll be with us when he's wanted at the end,
  For both his horse and he are mountain bred.

"He hails from Snowy River, up by Kosciusko's side,
  Where the hills are twice as steep and twice as rough;
Where a horse's hoofs strike firelight from the flint stones every
      stride.
  The man that holds his own is good enough.
And the Snowy River riders on the mountains make their home,
  Where the river runs those giant hills between;
I have seen full many horsemen since I first commenced to roam,
  But nowhere yet such horsemen have I seen."

So he went; they found the horses by the big mimosa clump,
  They raced away towards the mountain's brow,
And the old man gave his orders, "Boys, go at them from the
      jump,
  No use to try for fancy riding now.
And, Clancy, you must wheel them, try and wheel them to the
      right.
  Ride boldly, lad, and never fear the spills,
For never yet was rider that could keep the mob in sight,
  If once they gain the shelter of those hills."

So Clancy rode to wheel them – he was racing on the wing
  Where the best and boldest riders take their place,
And he raced his stock-horse past them, and he made the ranges
      ring
  With the stockwhip, as he met them face to face.
Then they halted for a moment, while he swung the dreaded
      lash,
  But they saw their well-loved mountain full in view,
And they charged beneath the stockwhip with a sharp and
      sudden dash,
  And off into the mountain scrub they flew.

Then fast the horsemen followed, where the gorges deep and
    black
    Resounded to the thunder of their tread,
And the stockwhips woke the echoes, and they fiercely answered
    back
    From cliffs and crags that beetled overhead.
And upward, ever upward, the wild horses held their way,
    Where mountain ash and kurrajong grew wide;
And the old man muttered fiercely, "We may bid the mob good
    day,
    No man can hold them down the other side."

When they reached the mountain's summit, even Clancy took a
    pull –
    It well might make the boldest hold their breath;
The wild hop scrub grew thickly, and the hidden ground was full
    Of wombat holes, and any slip was death.
But the man from Snowy River let the pony have his head,
    And he swung his stockwhip round and gave a cheer,
And he raced him down the mountain like a torrent down its bed,
    While the others stood and watched in very fear.

He sent the flint-stones flying, but the pony kept his feet,
    He cleared the fallen timber in his stride,
And the man from Snowy River never shifted in his seat –
    It was grand to see that mountain horseman ride.
Through the stringy barks and saplings, on the rough and broken
    ground,
    Down the hillside at a racing pace he went;
And he never drew the bridle till he landed safe and sound
    At the bottom of that terrible descent.

He was right among the horses as they climbed the farther hill,
    And the watchers on the mountain, standing mute,
Saw him ply the stockwhip fiercely; he was right among them
    still,
    As he raced across the clearing in pursuit.
Then they lost him for a moment, where two mountain gullies met
    In the ranges – but a final glimpse reveals
On a dim and distant hillside the wild horses racing yet,
    With the man from Snowy River at their heels.

And he ran them single-handed till their sides were white with
 foam;
 He followed like a bloodhound on their track,
Till they halted, cowed and beaten; then he turned their heads
 for home,
 And alone and unassisted brought them back.
But his hardy mountain pony he could scarcely raise a trot,
 He was blood from hip to shoulder from the spur;
But his pluck was still undaunted, and his courage fiery hot,
 For never yet was mountain horse a cur.

And down by Kosciusko, where the pine-clad ridges raise
 Their torn and rugged battlements on high,
Where the air is clear as crystal, and the white stars fairly blaze
 At midnight in the cold and frosty sky,
And where around the Overflow the reed-beds sweep and sway
 To the breezes, and the rolling plains are wide,
The Man from Snowy River is a household word today,
 And the stockmen tell the story of his ride.

Paul Revere's Ride

HENRY WADSWORTH LONGFELLOW

*Today Boston, like almost every other city, has a number of
high-rise blocks, but the Old North Church and the house
where Paul Revere lived with his family are still there. It takes
about ten minutes to walk between the two, and the distance
across the bridge to Charlestown is another thirty minutes. It is
easy to imagine the wariness and the excitement in the
community as they stood up for their rights against the British.
The urgency of the poem unconsciously increases the speed of
walking, so this is a good poem for a long, boring walk.*

Listen, my children, and you shall hear
Of the midnight ride of Paul Revere,
On the eighteenth of April, in Seventy-five;
Hardly a man is now alive
Who remembers that famous day and year.

He said to his friend, "If the British march
By land or sea from the town to-night,
Hang a lantern aloft in the belfry arch
Of the North Church tower as a signal light, –
One, if by land, and two, if by sea;
And I on the opposite shore will be
Ready to ride and spread the alarm
Through every Middlesex village and farm,
For the country folk to be up and to arm."
Then he said "Good-night," and with muffled oar
Silently row'd to the Charlestown shore,
Just as the moon rose over the bay,
Where swinging wide at her moorings lay
The *Somerset*, British man-of-war;
A phantom ship, with each mast and spar
Across the moon like a prison bar,
And a huge black hulk, that was magnified
By its own reflection in the tide.

Meanwhile his friend, through alley and street,
Wanders and watches with eager ears,
Till in the silence around him he hears
The muster of men at the barrack-door,
The sound of arms, and the tramp of feet,
And the measured tread of the grenadiers
Marching down to their boats on the shore.

Then he climb'd the tower of the Old North Church,
By the wooden stairs, with stealthy tread,
To the belfry-chamber overhead,
And started the pigeons from their perch
On the sombre rafters, that round him made
Masses of moving shapes of shade, –
By the trembling ladder, steep and tall,
To the highest window in the wall,
Where he paused to listen and look down
A moment on the roofs of the town,
And the moonlight flowing over all.

Beneath, in the churchyard, lay the dead,
In their night-encampment on the hill,
Wrapp'd in silence so deep and still
That he could hear, like a sentinel's tread,
The watchful night-wind, as it went
Creeping along from tent to tent,
And seeming to whisper, "All is well!"
A moment only he feels the spell
Of the place and the hour, and the secret dread
Of the lonely belfry and the dead;
For suddenly all his thoughts are bent
On a shadowy something far away,
Where the river widens to meet the bay,
A line of black that bends and floats
On the rising tide like a bridge of boats.

Meanwhile, impatient to mount and ride,
Booted and spurr'd, with a heavy stride
On the opposite shore walk'd Paul Revere.
Now he patted his horse's side,
Now he gazed at the landscape far and near,
Then, impetuous, stamp'd the earth,
And turn'd and tighten'd his saddle-girth;
But mostly he watch'd with eager search
The belfry-tower of the Old North Church,
As it rose above the graves on the hill,
Lonely and spectral and sombre and still.
And lo! as he looks, on the belfry's height
A glimmer, and then a gleam of light!
He springs to the saddle, the bridle he turns,
But lingers and gazes, till full on his sight
A second lamp in the belfry burns.

A hurry of hoofs in a village street,
A shape in the moonlight, a bulk in the dark,
And beneath, from the pebbles, in passing, a spark
Struck out by a steed flying fearless and fleet:
That was all; and yet, through the gloom and the light,
The fate of a nation was riding that night;
And the spark struck out by that steed in his flight
Kindled the land into flame with its heat.

He had left the village and mounted the steep,
And beneath him, tranquil and broad and deep,
Is the Mystic, meeting the ocean tides,
And under the alders that skirts its edge,
Now soft on the sand, now loud on the ledge,
Is heard the tramp of his steed as he rides.

It was twelve by the village clock
When he crossed the bridge into Medford town.
He heard the crowing of the cock,
And the barking of the farmer's dog,
And felt the damp of the river fog,
That rises after the sun goes down.

It was one by the village clock
When he galloped into Lexington.
He saw the gilded weathercock
Swim in the moonlight as he pass'd,
And the meeting-house windows, blank and bare,
Gaze at him with a spectral glare,
As if they already stood aghast
At the bloody work they would look upon.

It was two by the village clock
When he came to the bridge in Concord town.
He heard the bleating of the flock,
And the twitter of birds among the trees,
And felt the breath of the morning breeze
Blowing over the meadows brown.

And one was safe and asleep in his bed
Who at the bridge would be first to fall,
Who that day would be lying dead,
Pierced by a British musket-ball.

You know the rest; in the books you have read,
How the British regulars fired and fled, –
How the farmers gave them ball for ball,
From behind each fence and farmyard wall,
Chasing the red-coats down the lane,
Then crossing the fields to emerge again
Under the trees at the turn of the road,
And only pausing to fire and load.

So through the night rode Paul Revere,
And so through the night went his cry of alarm
To every Middlesex village and farm, –
A cry of defiance, and not of fear,
A voice in the darkness, a knock at the door,
And a word that shall echo for evermore!
For, borne on the night-wind of the past,
Through all our history, to the last,
In the hour of darkness, and peril, and need,
The people will waken and listen to hear
The hurrying hoof-beats of that steed,
And the midnight message of Paul Revere.

The Rolling English Road

G. K. CHESTERTON

*It's fun to read this with a map of England beside you. I was
only recently introduced to this poem by some friends of mine,
and find it a delightful view of pleasantly convoluted country
lanes. But it is also a look at our journey through life and its
inevitable end.*

Before the Roman came to Rye or out to Severn strode,
The rolling English drunkard made the rolling English road.
A reeling road, a rolling road, that rambles round the shire,
And after him the parson ran, the sexton and the squire;
A merry road, a mazy road, and such as we did tread
The night we went to Birmingham by way of Beachy Head.

I knew no harm of Bonaparte and plenty of the Squire,
And for to fight the Frenchman I did not much desire;
But I did bash their baggonets because they came arrayed
To straighten out the crooked road an English drunkard made,
Where you and I went down the lane with ale-mugs in our
      hands,
The night we went to Glastonbury by way of Goodwin Sands.

His sins they were forgiven him; or why do flowers run
Behind him; and the hedges all strengthening in the sun?
The wild thing went from left to right and knew not which was
    which,
But the wild rose was above him when they found him in the
    ditch.
God pardon us, nor harden us; we did not see so clear
The night we went to Bannockburn by way of Brighton Pier.

My friends, we will not go again or ape an ancient rage,
Or stretch the folly of our youth to be the shame of age,
But walk with clearer eyes and ears this path that wandereth,
And see undrugged in evening light the decent inn of death;
For there is good news yet to hear and fine things to be seen,
Before we go to Paradise by way of Kensal Green.

The Speech Before Harfleur

WILLIAM SHAKESPEARE
From *Henry V*, Act 3 Scene 1

*Much of Shakespeare's verse can be said aloud in isolation from
the rest of the particular play, and this is one such passage. It's
a good one for a walk which is going to result in being
somewhere you don't particularly want to be, like school or the
dentist.*

Once more unto the breach, dear friends, once more;
Or close the wall up with our English dead!
In peace there's nothing so becomes a man,
As modest stillness and humility:
But when the blast of war blows in our ears,
Then imitate the action of the tiger;
Stiffen the sinews, summon up the blood,
Disguise fair nature with hard-favoured rage,
Then lend the eye a terrible aspect;
Let it pry through the portage of the head,
Like the brass cannon: let the brow o'erwhelm it,
As fearfully as doth a galled rock
O'erhang and jutty his confounded base
Swilled with the wild and wasteful ocean.
Now set the teeth, and stretch the nostril wide;
Hold hard the breath, and bend up every spirit
To his full height! – On, on, you noblest English!
Whose blood is fet from fathers of warproof;
Fathers that, like so many Alexanders,
Have in these parts from morn till even fought,
And sheathed their swords for lack of argument.
Dishonour not your mothers: now attest
That those whom you called fathers did beget you!
Be copy now to men of grosser blood,
And teach them how to war! – And you, good yeomen,
Whose limbs were made in England, show us here
The mettle of your pasture; let us swear
That you are worth your breeding, which I doubt not;
For there is none of you so mean and base
That hath not noble lustre in your eyes.
I see you stand like greyhounds in the slips,
Straining upon the start. The game's afoot;
Follow your spirit: and, upon this charge,
Cry – God for Harry! England and Saint George!

The Tale of Custard the Dragon

OGDEN NASH

The next time you are going for a walk with a small friend whose legs are not as long as yours, try telling this story. The easy, short rhyming lines and the ridiculous situation Belinda gets herself into will take your minds off the walk and make it a far more enjoyable occasion than you thought it would be.

Belinda lived in a little white house,
With a little black kitten and a little grey mouse,
And a little yellow dog and a little red wagon,
And a realio, trulio, little pet dragon.

Now the name of the little black kitten was Ink,
And the little grey mouse, she called her Blink,
And the little yellow dog was sharp as Mustard,
But the dragon was a coward, and she called him Custard.

Custard the dragon had big sharp teeth,
And spikes on top of him and scales underneath,
Mouth like a fireplace, chimney for a nose,
And realio, trulio daggers on his toes.

Belinda was as brave as a barrelful of bears,
And Ink and Blink chased lions down the stairs,
Mustard was as brave as a tiger in a rage,
But Custard cried for a nice safe cage.

Belinda tickled him, she tickled him unmerciful,
Ink, Blink and Mustard, they rudely called him Percival,
They all sat laughing in the little red wagon
At the realio, trulio, cowardly dragon.

Belinda giggled till she shook the house,
And Blink said *Weeek!*, which is giggling for a mouse,
Ink and Mustard rudely asked his age,
When Custard cried for a nice safe cage.

Suddenly, suddenly they heard a nasty sound,
And Mustard growled, and they all looked around.
Meowch! cried Ink, and Ooh! cried Belinda,
For there was a pirate, climbing in the winda.

Pistol in his left hand, pistol in his right,
And he held in his teeth a cutlass bright;
His beard was black, one leg was wood.
It was clear that the pirate meant no good.

Belinda paled, and she cried Help! Help!
But Mustard fled with a terrified yelp,
Ink trickled down to the bottom of the household,
And little mouse Blink strategically mouseholed.

But up jumped Custard, snorting like an engine,
Clashed his tail like irons in a dungeon,
With a clatter and a clank and a jangling squirm
He went at the pirate like a robin at a worm.

The pirate gaped at Belinda's dragon,
And gulped some grog from his pocket flagon,
He fired two bullets, but they didn't hit,
And Custard gobbled him, every bit.

Belinda embraced him, Mustard licked him;
No one mourned for his pirate victim.
Ink and Blink in glee did gyrate
Around the dragon that ate the pyrate.

Belinda still lives in her little white house,
With her little black kitten and her little grey mouse,
And her little yellow dog and her little red wagon,
And her realio, trulio, little pet dragon.

Belinda is as brave as a barrelful of bears,
And Ink and Blink chase lions down the stairs,
Mustard is as brave as a tiger in a rage,
But Custard keeps crying for a nice safe cage.

A Visit from St. Nicholas

CLEMENT CLARKE MOORE

The best time for this poem is Christmas, but it does need to be practised at other times too. Perhaps coming home tired from shopping on a wet, cold December evening would be a good time as you could cheer everyone up by reminding them of what is to come.

'Twas the night before Christmas, when all through the house
Not a creature was stirring, not even a mouse;
The stockings were hung by the chimney with care,
In hopes that St. Nicholas soon would be there;
The children were nestled all snug in their beds,
While visions of sugar-plums danced in their heads;
And mamma in her kerchief, and I in my cap,
Had just settled our brains for a long winter nap –
When out on the lawn there arose such a clatter,
I sprang from my bed to see what was the matter.
Away to the window I flew like a flash,
Tore open the shutters and threw up the sash.
The moon, on the breast of the new-fallen snow,
Gave a lustre of midday to objects below;
When what to my wondering eyes should appear
But a miniature sleigh and eight tiny reindeer,
With a little old driver, so lively and quick,
I knew in a moment it must be St. Nick.
More rapid than eagles his coursers they came,
And he whistled, and shouted, and called them by name:
"Now, Dasher! now, Dancer! now, Prancer and Vixen!
On, Comet! on, Cupid! on, Donder and Blitzen!
To the top of the porch, to the top of the wall!
Now, dash away, dash away, dash away all!"
As dry leaves that before the wild hurricane fly,
When they meet with an obstacle, mount to the sky,
So up to the house-top the coursers they flew,
With the sleigh full of toys – and St. Nicholas too.
And then in a twinkling I heard on the roof
The prancing and pawing of each little hoof.
As I drew in my head, and was turning around,
Down the chimney St. Nicholas came with a bound.
He was dressed all in fur from his head to his foot,
And his clothes were all tarnished with ashes and soot;

A bundle of toys he had flung on his back,
And he looked like a peddler just opening his pack.
His eyes how they twinkled! his dimples how merry!
His cheeks were like roses, his nose like a cherry;
His droll little mouth was drawn up like a bow,
And the beard on his chin was as white as the snow.
The stump of a pipe he held tight in his teeth,
And the smoke it encircled his head like a wreath.
He had a broad face and a little round belly
That shook, when he laughed, like a bowl full of jelly.
He was chubby and plump, – a right jolly old elf,
And I laughed, when I saw him, in spite of myself.
A wink of his eye and a twist of his head
Soon gave me to know I had nothing to dread.
He spoke not a word, but went straight to his work,
And filled all the stockings; then turned with a jerk,
And laying his finger aside of his nose,
And giving a nod, up the chimney he rose.
He sprang to his sleigh, to his team gave a whistle,
And away they all flew like the down of a thistle;
But I heard him exclaim, ere he drove out of sight,
"Happy Christmas to all, and to all a good night!"

For Visiting Relatives and Other Family Occasions

The Ballad of Agincourt

MICHAEL DRAYTON

War is an act of aggression, yet sometimes a poet can lift the description of a war into the realms of lyrical poetry. This is a good poem for occasions where family memories are being scoured for tales of heroism. Here, England is the hero.

Fair stood the wind for France
    When we our sails advance,
Nor now to prove our chance
    Longer will tarry;
But putting to the main
At Caux, the mouth of Seine,
With all his martial train,
    Landed King Harry.

And taking many a fort,
    Furnished in warlike sort,
Marcheth toward Agincourt
    In happy hour;
Skirmishing day by day
With those that stopped his way
Where the French general lay
    With all his power.

Which, in his height of pride,
    King Henry to deride,
His ransom to provide
    Unto him sending;
Which he neglects the while,
As from a nation vile,
Yet, with an angry smile
    Their fall portending.

And, turning to his men,
    Quoth our brave Henry then:
Though they to one be ten,
    Be not amazèd;
Yet have we well begun –
Battles so bravely won
Have ever to the sun
    By fame been raisèd.

And for myself, quoth he,
    This my full rest shall be:
England ne'er mourn for me,
    Nor more esteem me:
Victor I will remain,
Or on this earth lie slain;
Never shall she sustain
    Loss to redeem me.

Poitiers and Creçy tell,
    When most their pride did swell,
Under our swords they fell:
    No less our skill is
Than when our grandsire great,
Claiming the regal seat,
By many a warlike feat
    Lopped the French lilies.

The Duke of York so dread
    The eager vaward led;
With the main Henry sped
    Amongst his henchmen.
Exeter had the rear,
A braver man not there:
O Lord, how hot they were
    On the false Frenchmen!

They now to fight are gone;
    Armour on armour shone;
Drum now to drum did groan:
    To hear was wonder;
That with the cries they make
The very earth did shake;
Trumpet to trumpet spake,
    Thunder to thunder.

Well it thine age became,
    O noble Erpingham,
Which didst the signal aim
    To our hid forces!
When, from a meadow by,
Like a storm suddenly,
The English archery
    Struck the French horses.

With Spanish yew so strong,
Arrows a cloth-yard long,
That like to serpents stung,
    Piercing the weather;
None from his fellow starts,
But playing manly parts,
And, like true English hearts,
    Stuck close together.

When down their bows they threw,
And forth their bilboes drew,
And on the French they flew,
    Not one was tardy:
Arms were from shoulders sent;
Scalps to the teeth were rent;
Down the French peasants went;
    Our men were hardy.

This while our noble king,
His broadsword brandishing,
Down the French host did ding,
    As to o'erwhelm it;
And many a deep wound rent
His arms with blood besprent,
And many a cruel dent
    Bruised his helmet.

Gloster, that duke so good,
Next of the royal blood
For famous England stood,
    With his brave brother
Clarence, in steel so bright,
Though but a maiden knight,
Yet in that furious fight
    Scarce such another.

Warwick in blood did wade;
Oxford the foe invade,
And cruel slaughter made,
    Still as they ran up.
Suffolk his axe did ply;
Beaumont and Willoughby
Bare them right doughtily,
    Ferrers and Fanhope.

Upon Saint Crispin's day
Fought was this noble fray,
Which fame did not delay
    To England to carry.
O, when shall Englishmen
With such acts fill a pen,
Or England breed again
    Such a King Harry?

Elegy Written in a Country Churchyard

THOMAS GRAY

All your older relatives will know this, but they will not expect you to be able to recite it. Nor, if they ask you to recite will they be expecting a poem as long as this. It takes courage and a good memory to commit it to heart, but the effort is worth the amazed looks on the faces of your relatives.

The Curfew tolls the knell of parting day,
    The lowing herd wind slowly o'er the lea,
The plowman homeward plods his weary way,
    And leaves the world to darkness and to me.

Now fades the glimmering landscape on the sight,
    And all the air a solemn stillness holds,
Save where the beetle wheels his droning flight,
    And drowsy tinklings lull the distant folds;

Save that from yonder ivy-mantled tow'r
    The moping owl does to the moon complain
Of such as, wand'ring near her secret bower,
    Molest her ancient solitary reign.

Beneath those rugged elms, that yew-tree's shade,
    Where heaves the turf in many a mould'ring heap,
Each in his narrow cell for ever laid,
    The rude Forefathers of the hamlet sleep.

The breezy call of incense-breathing Morn,
    The swallow twitt'ring from the straw-built shed,
The cock's shrill clarion, or the echoing horn,
    No more shall rouse them from their lowly bed.

For them no more the blazing hearth shall burn,
    Or busy housewife ply her evening care:
No children run to lisp their sire's return,
    Or climb his knees the envied kiss to share.

Oft did the harvest to their sickle yield,
    Their furrow oft the stubborn glebe has broke:
How jocund did they drive their team afield!
    How bow'd the woods beneath their sturdy stroke!

Let not Ambition mock their useful toil,
    Their homely joys, and destiny obscure;
Nor Grandeur hear with a disdainful smile
    The short and simple annals of the poor.

The boast of heraldry, the pomp of pow'r,
    And all that beauty, all that wealth e'er gave,
Awaits alike th' inevitable hour:
    The paths of glory lead but to the grave.

Nor you, ye Proud, impute to These the fault,
    If Memory o'er their Tomb no Trophies raise,
Where through the long-drawn aisle and fretted vault
    The pealing anthem swells the note of praise.

Can storied urn or animated bust
    Back to its mansion call the fleeting breath?
Can Honour's voice provoke the silent dust,
    Or Flatt'ry soothe the dull cold ear of death?

Perhaps in this neglected spot is laid
    Some heart once pregnant with celestial fire;
Hands, that the rod of empire might have sway'd,
    Or waked to ecstasy the living lyre.

But Knowledge to their eyes her ample page
   Rich with the spoils of time did ne'er unroll;
Chill Penury repress'd their noble rage,
   And froze the genial current of the soul.

Full many a gem of purest ray serene
   The dark unfathom'd caves of ocean bear:
Full many a flower is born to blush unseen,
   And waste its sweetness on the desert air.

Some village Hampden that with dauntless breast
   The little tyrant of his fields withstood,
Some mute inglorious Milton, here may rest,
   Some Cromwell guiltless of his country's blood.

Th' applause of list'ning senates to command,
   The threats of pain and ruin to despise,
To scatter plenty o'er a smiling land,
   And read their history in a nation's eyes,

Their lot forbade: nor circumscribed alone
   Their growing virtues, but their crimes confined;
Forbade to wade through slaughter to a throne,
   And shut the gates of mercy on mankind,

The struggling pangs of conscious truth to hide,
   To quench the blushes of ingenuous shame,
Or heap the shrine of Luxury and Pride
   With incense kindled at the Muse's flame.

Far from the madding crowd's ignoble strife
   Their sober wishes never learn'd to stray;
Along the cool sequester'd vale of life
   They kept the noiseless tenor of their way.

Yet ev'n these bones from insult to protect
   Some frail memorial still erected nigh,
With uncouth rhymes and shapeless sculpture deck'd,
   Implores the passing tribute of a sigh.

Their name, their years, spelt by th' unletter'd muse,
   The place of fame and elegy supply:
And many a holy text around she strews,
   That teach the rustic moralist to die.

For who, to dumb Forgetfulness a prey,
   This pleasing anxious being e'er resign'd,
Left the warm precincts of the cheerful day,
   Nor cast one longing ling'ring look behind?

On some fond breast the parting soul relies,
   Some pious drops the closing eye requires;
E'en from the tomb the voice of Nature cries,
   E'en in our Ashes live their wonted Fires.

For thee, who, mindful of th' unhonour'd dead,
   Dost in these lines their artless tale relate;
If chance, by lonely contemplation led,
   Some kindred spirit shall inquire thy fate,

Haply some hoary-headed Swain may say,
   "Oft have we seen him at the peep of dawn
Brushing with hasty steps the dews away
   To meet the sun upon the upland lawn.

"There at the foot of yonder nodding beech
   That wreathes its old fantastic roots so high,
His listless length at noontide would he stretch,
   And pore upon the brook that babbles by.

"Hard by yon wood, now smiling as in scorn,
    Mutt'ring his wayward fancies he would rove,
Now drooping, woeful wan, like one forlorn,
    Or crazed with care, or cross'd in hopeless love.

"One morn I miss'd him on the custom'd hill,
    Along the heath and near his fav'rite tree;
Another came, not yet beside the rill,
    Nor up the lawn, nor at the wood was he;

"The next with dirges due in sad array
    Slow through the church-way path we saw him borne.
Approach and read (for thou canst read) the lay
    Graved on the stone beneath yon aged thorn."

THE EPITAPH
Here rests his head upon the lap of Earth
    A Youth to Fortune and to Fame unknown,.
Fair Science frown'd not on his humble birth,
    And Melancholy mark'd him for her own.

Large was his bounty, and his soul sincere,
    Heav'n did a recompense as largely send:
He gave to Mis'ry all he had, a tear,
    He gain'd from Heav'n ('twas all he wish'd) a friend.

No farther seek his merits to disclose,
    Or draw his frailties from their dread abode,
(There they alike in trembling hope repose,)
    The bosom of his Father and his God.

The Famous Tay Whale

WILLIAM McGONAGALL

McGonagall was a dreadful poet! His lines don't scan and some rhyme is suspect – but there is something compelling about the way he tortures language to tell a story. This is ideal for a lighthearted family occasion when everyone is a bit mellow and wanting to laugh.

'Twas in the month of December, and in the year 1883,
That a monster whale came to Dundee,
Resolved for a few days to sport and play,
And devour the small fishes in the silvery Tay.

So the monster whale did sport and play
Among the innocent little fishes in the beautiful Tay,
Until he was seen by some men one day,
And they resolved to catch him without delay.

When it came to be known a whale was seen in the Tay,
Some men began to talk and to say,
We must try and catch this monster of a whale,
So come on, brave boys, and never say fail.

Then the people together in crowds did run,
Resolved to capture the whale and to have some fun!
So small boats were launched on the silvery Tay,
While the monster of the deep did sport and play.

Oh! it was a most fearful and beautiful sight,
To see it lashing the water with its tail all its might,
And making the water ascend like a shower of hail,
With one lash of its ugly and mighty tail.

Then the water did descend on the men in the boats,
Which wet their trousers and also their coats;
But it only made them the more determined to catch the whale,
But the whale shook at them his tail.

Then the whale began to puff and to blow,
While the men and the boats after him did go,
Armed well with harpoons for the fray,
Which they fired at him without dismay.

And they laughed and grinned just like wild baboons,
While they fired at him their sharp harpoons:
But when struck with the harpoons he dived below,
Which filled his pursuers' hearts with woe:

Because they guessed they had lost a prize,
Which caused the tears to well up in their eyes;
And in that their anticipations were only right,
Because he sped on to Stonehaven with all his might:

And was first seen by the crew of a Gourdon fishing boat,
Which they thought was a big coble upturned afloat;
But when they drew near they saw it was a whale,
So they resolved to tow it ashore without fail.

So they got a rope from each boat tied round his tail,
And landed their burden at Stonehaven without fail;
And when the people saw it their voices they did raise,
Declaring that the brave fishermen deserved great praise.

And my opinion is that God sent the whale in time of need,
No matter what other people may think or what is their creed;
I know fishermen in general are often very poor,
And God in His goodness sent it to drive poverty from their
       door.

So Mr John Wood has bought it for two hundred and twenty-six
       pound,
And has brought it to Dundee all safe and all sound;
Which measures 40 feet in length from the snout to the tail,
So I advise the people far and near to see it without fail.

Then hurrah! for the mighty monster whale,
Which has got 17 feet 4 inches from tip to tip of a tail!
Which can be seen for a sixpence or a shilling,
That is to say, if the people all are willing.

Friends, Romans, Countrymen

WILLIAM SHAKESPEARE
From *Julius Cæsar*, Act 3 Scene 2

Almost everyone who has ever been to school will, at some time, have been exposed to these lines. An opportunity for all thespians to show their skill at declaiming Shakespeare.

Friends, Romans, countrymen, lend me your ears;
I come to bury Cæsar, not to praise him.
The evil that men do lives after them,
The good is oft interred with their bones;
So let it be with Cæsar. The noble Brutus
Hath told you Cæsar was ambitious;
If it were so, it was a grievous fault,
And grievously hath Cæsar answered it.
Here, under leave of Brutus and the rest, –
For Brutus is an honourable man;
So are they all, all honourable men, –
Come I to speak in Cæsar's funeral.
He was my friend, faithful and just to me;
But Brutus says he was ambitious;
And Brutus is an honourable man.
He hath brought many captives home to Rome,
Whose ransoms did the general coffers fill:
Did this in Cæsar seem ambitious?
When that the poor have cried, Cæsar hath wept;
Ambition should be made of sterner stuff:
Yet Brutus says he was ambitious;
And Brutus is an honourable man.
You all did see that on the Lupercal
I thrice presented him a kingly crown,
Which he did thrice refuse: was this ambition?
Yet Brutus says he was ambitious;
And, sure, he is an honourable man.
I speak not to disprove what Brutus spoke,
But here I am to speak what I do know.
You all did love him once, not without cause:
What cause withholds you then to mourn for him?
O judgment! thou art fled to brutish beasts,
And men have lost their reason. Bear with me;
My heart is in the coffin there with Cæsar,
And I must pause till it come back to me.

The Highwayman ALFRED NOYES

*Oh, the shiver of expectation that runs down the spine when
the first lines of this poem are uttered in a darkened room.
There's intrigue, mystery, romance and death in these famous
lines.*

Part One

The wind was a torrent of darkness among the gusty trees,
The moon was a ghostly galleon tossed upon cloudy seas,
The road was a ribbon of moonlight over the purple moor,
And the highwayman came riding –
      Riding – riding –
The highwayman came riding, up to the old inn-door.

He'd a French cocked-hat on his forehead, a bunch of lace at his
    chin,
A coat of the claret velvet, and breeches of brown doeskin:
They fitted with never a wrinkle; his boots were up to the thigh!
And he rode with a jewelled twinkle,
      His pistol butts a-twinkle,
His rapier hilt a-twinkle, under the jewelled sky.

Over the cobbles he clattered and clashed in the dark inn-yard,
And he tapped with his whip on the shutters, but all was locked
    and barred:
He whistled a tune to the window; and who should be waiting
    there
But the landlord's black-eyed daughter,
      Bess, the landlord's daughter,
Plaiting a dark red love-knot into her long black hair.

And dark in the dark old inn-yard a stable-wicket creaked
Where Tim, the ostler, listened; his face was white and peaked,
His eyes were hollows of madness, his hair like mouldy hay;
But he loved the landlord's daughter,
      The landlord's red-lipped daughter:
Dumb as a dog he listened, and he heard the robber say –

"One kiss, my bonny sweetheart, I'm after a prize tonight,
But I shall be back with the yellow gold before the morning light.
Yet if they press me sharply, and harry me through the day,
Then look for me by moonlight,
      Watch for me by moonlight:
I'll come to thee by moonlight, though Hell should bar the way."

He rose upright in the stirrups, he scarce could reach her hand;
But she loosened her hair i' the casement! His face burnt like a
    brand
As the black cascade of perfume came tumbling over his breast;
And he kissed its waves in the moonlight,
       (Oh, sweet black waves in the moonlight)
Then he tugged at his reins in the moonlight, and galloped away
     to the West.

Part Two

He did not come in the dawning; he did not come at noon;
And out of the tawny sunset, before the rise o' the moon,
When the road was a gypsy's ribbon, looping the purple moor,
A red-coat troop came marching –
     Marching – marching –
King George's men came marching, up to the old inn-door.

They said no word to the landlord, they drank his ale instead;
But they gagged his daughter and bound her to the foot of her
    narrow bed.
Two of them knelt at her casement, with muskets at the side!
There was death at every window;
     And Hell at one dark window;
For Bess could see, through her casement, the road that *he* would
    ride.

They had tied her up to attention, with many a sniggering jest:
They had bound a musket beside her, with the barrel beneath her
    breast!
"Now keep good watch!" and they kissed her.
     She heard the dead man say –
Look for me by moonlight;
    Watch for me by moonlight;
I'll come to thee by moonlight, though Hell should bar the way!

She twisted her hands behind her; but all the knots held good!
She writhed her hands till her fingers were wet with sweat or
    blood!
They stretched and strained in the darkness, and the hours
    crawled by like years;
Till, now, on the stroke of midnight,
        Cold, on the stroke of midnight,
The tip of one finger touched it! The trigger at least was hers!

The tip of one finger touched it; she strove no more for the rest!
Up, she stood up to attention, with the barrel beneath her breast,
She would not risk their hearing: she would not strive again;
For the road lay bare in the moonlight,
        Blank and bare in the moonlight;
And the blood of her veins in the moonlight throbbed to her
    Love's refrain.

Tlot-tlot, tlot-tlot! Had they heard it? The horse-hoofs ringing
    clear –
Tlot-tlot, tlot-tlot, in the distance? Were they deaf that they did
    not hear?
Down the ribbon of moonlight, over the brow of the hill,
The highwayman came riding,
        Riding, riding!
The red-coats looked to their priming! She stood up straight and
    still!

Tlot-tlot, in the frosty silence! *Tlot-tlot* in the echoing night!
Nearer he came and nearer! Her face was like a light!
Her eyes grew wide for a moment; she drew one last deep
    breath,
Then her finger moved in the moonlight,
        Her musket shattered the moonlight,
Shattered her breast in the moonlight and warned him – with
    her death.

He turned; he spurred him westward; he did not know who
      stood
Bowed with her head o'er the musket, drenched with her own
      red blood!
Not till the dawn he heard it, and slowly blanched to hear
How Bess, the landlord's daughter,
        The landlord's black-eyed daughter,
Had watched for her Love in the moonlight; and died in the
      darkness there.

Back he spurred like a madman, shrieking a curse to the sky,
With the white road smoking behind him, and his rapier
      brandished high!
Blood-red were his spurs i' the golden noon; wine-red was his
      velvet coat;
When they shot him down on the highway,
        Down like a dog on the highway,
And he lay in his blood on the highway, with the bunch of lace at
      his throat.

*   *   *   *   *

And still of a winter's night, they say, when the wind is in the
      trees,
When the moon is a ghostly galleon tossed upon cloudy seas,
When the road is a ribbon of moonlight over the purple moor,
A highwayman comes riding –
        Riding – riding –
A highwayman comes riding, up to the old inn-door.

Over the cobbles he clatters and clangs in the dark inn-yard;
And he taps with his whip on the shutters, but all is locked and
      barred:
He whistles a tune to the window, and who should be waiting
      there
But the landlord's black-eyed daughter,
        Bess, the landlord's daughter,
Plaiting a dark red love-knot into her long black hair.

How They Brought the Good News From Ghent to Aix

ROBERT BROWNING

This is very dramatic if the reading or reciting is shared. A hushed tone is best for the narrative, so that the individual voices shout out the speech. It's an exciting poem, full of imagery and urgency.

I sprang to the stirrup, and Joris, and he;
I galloped, Dirck galloped, we galloped all three;
"Good speed!" cried the watch, as the gate bolts undrew,
"Speed!" echoed the wall to us galloping through;
Behind shut the postern, the lights sank to rest,
And into the midnight we galloped abreast.

Not a word to each other; we kept the great pace
Neck by neck, stride by stride, never changing our place;
I turned in my saddle and made its girths tight,
Then shortened each stirrup, and set the pique right,
Rebuckled the cheek-strap, chained slacker the bit,
Nor galloped less steadily Roland a whit.

'Twas moonset at starting; but while we drew near
Lokeren, the cocks crew and twilight dawned clear;
At Boom, a great yellow star came out to see;
At Düffeld, 'twas morning as plain as could be;
And from Mecheln church-steeple we heard the half-chime,
So, Joris broke silence with, "Yet there is time!"

At Aershot, up leaped of a sudden the sun,
And against him the cattle stood black every one,
To stare thro' the mist at us galloping past,
And I saw my stout galloper Roland at last,
With resolute shoulders, each butting away
The haze, as some bluff river headland its spray:

And his low head and crest, just one sharp ear bent back
For my voice, and the other pricked out on his track;
And one eye's black intelligence, – ever the glance
O'er its white edge at me, his own master askance!
And the thick heavy spume-flakes which aye and anon
His fierce lips shook upwards in galloping on.

By Hasselt, Dirck groaned; and cried Joris, "Stay spur!
Your Roos galloped bravely, the fault's not in her,
We'll remember at Aix" – for one heard the quick wheeze
Of her chest, saw the stretched neck and staggering knees,
And sunk tail, and horrible heave of the flank,
As down on her haunches she shuddered and sank.

So, we were left galloping, Joris and I,
Past Looz and past Tongres, no cloud in the sky;
The broad sun above laughed a pitiless laugh,
'Neath our feet broke the brittle bright stubble like chaff;
Till over by Dalhem a dome-spire sprang white,
And "Gallop," gasped Joris, "for Aix is in sight!"

"How they'll greet us!" – and all in a moment his roan
Rolled neck and croup over, lay dead as a stone;
And there was my Roland to bear the whole weight
Of the news which alone could save Aix from her fate,
With his nostrils like pits full of blood to the brim,
And with circles of red for his eye-sockets' rim.

Then I cast loose my buffcoat, each holster let fall,
Shook off both my jack-boots, let go belt and all,
Stood up in the stirrup, leaned, patted his ear,
Called my Roland his pet-name, my horse without peer;
Clapped my hands, laughed and sang, any noise, bad or good,
Till at length into Aix Roland galloped and stood.

And all I remember is – friends flocking round
As I sat with his head 'twixt my knees on the ground;
And no voice but was praising this Roland of mine,
As I poured down his throat our last measure of wine,
Which (the burgesses voted by common consent)
Was no more than his due who brought good news from Ghent.

The Inchcape Rock

ROBERT SOUTHEY

*Evil deeds abound in legend and the dastardly deed of Sir
Ralph becomes his own epitaph. A good poem for grandfathers
and greatuncles who are always telling you moral tales in order
to keep you under control.*

No stir in the air, no stir in the sea –
The ship was as still as she could be;
Her sails from heaven received no motion;
Her keel was steady in the ocean.

Without either sign or sound of their shock,
The waves flowed over the Inchcape rock;
So little they rose, so little they fell,
They did not move the Inchcape bell.

The holy Abbot of Aberbrothok
Had placed that bell on the Inchcape rock;
On a buoy in the storm it floated and swung
And over the waves its warning rung.

When the rock was hid by the surges' swell,
The mariners heard the warning bell;
And then they knew the perilous rock,
And blessed the Abbot of Aberbrothok.

The sun in heaven was shining gay –
All things were joyful on that day;
The sea-birds screamed as they wheeled around,
And there was joyance in their sound.

The buoy of the Inchcape bell was seen,
A darker speck on the ocean green;
Sir Ralph, the rover, walked his deck,
And he fixed his eyes on the darker speck.

His eye was on the bell and float:
Quoth he, "My men, put out the boat;
And row me to the Inchcape rock,
And I'll plague the priest of Aberbrothok."

The boat is lowered, the boatmen row,
And to the Inchcape rock they go;
Sir Ralph bent over from the boat,
And cut the warning bell from the float.

Down sank the bell with a gurgling sound;
The bubbles rose, and burst around.
Quoth Sir Ralph, "The next who comes to the rock
Will not bless the Abbot of Aberbrothok."

Sir Ralph, the rover, sailed away –
He scoured the seas for many a day;
And now, grown rich with plundered store,
He steers his course to Scotland's shore.

So thick a haze o'erspreads the sky
They cannot see the sun on high;
The wind hath blown a gale all day;
At evening it hath died away.

On the deck the rover takes his stand;
So dark it is they see no land.
Quoth Sir Ralph, "It will be lighter soon,
For there is the dawn of the rising moon."

"Canst hear," said one, "the breakers roar?
For yonder, methinks, should be the shore.
Now where we are I cannot tell,
But I wish we could hear the Inchcape bell."

They hear no sound; the swell is strong;
Though the wind hath fallen, they drift along;
Till the vessel strikes with a shivering shock –
O Christ! it is the Inchcape rock!

Sir Ralph, the rover, tore his hair;
He cursed himself in his despair.
The waves rush in on every side;
The ship is sinking beneath the tide.

But ever in his dying fear
One dreadful sound he seemed to hear –
A sound as if with the Inchcape bell
The Devil below was ringing his knell.

Journey of the Magi   T. S. ELIOT

After Christmas dinner is cleared away and everyone has had a
rest is the right time for this quiet reflective poem of the
coming of the three wise men. Not a joyous poem but one in
which prophecy has a strong voice.

"A cold coming we had of it,
Just the worst time of the year
For a journey, and such a long journey:
The ways deep and the weather sharp,
The very dead of winter."
And the camels galled, sore-footed, refractory,
Lying down in the melting snow.
There were times we regretted
The summer palaces on slopes, the terraces,
And the silken girls bringing sherbet.
Then the camel men cursing and grumbling
And running away, and wanting their liquor and women,
And the night-fires going out, and the lack of shelters,
And the cities hostile and the towns unfriendly
And the villages dirty and charging high prices:
A hard time we had of it.
At the end we preferred to travel all night,
Sleeping in snatches,
With the voices singing in our ears, saying
That this was all folly.

Then at dawn we came down to a temperate valley,
Wet, below the snow line, smelling of vegetation;
With a running stream and a water-mill beating the darkness,
And three trees on the low sky,
And an old white horse galloped away in the meadow.
Then we came to a tavern with vine-leaves over the lintel,
Six hands at an open door dicing for pieces of silver,
And feet kicking the empty wine-skins.
But there was no information, and so we continued
And arrived at evening, not a moment too soon
Finding the place; it was (you may say) satisfactory.

All this was a long time ago, I remember,
And I would do it again, but set down
This set down
This: were we led all that way for
Birth or Death? There was a Birth, certainly,
We had evidence and no doubt. I had seen birth and death,
But had thought they were different; this Birth was
Hard and bitter agony for us, like Death, our death.
We returned to our places, these Kingdoms,
But no longer at ease here, in the old dispensation,
With an alien people clutching their gods.
I should be glad of another death.

Kubla Khan SAMUEL TAYLOR COLERIDGE

A romantic poem well suited to family occasions such as the after-wedding let-down when the bride and groom have left. With everyone in their best clothes, the teapot on the table, shoes kicked across the floor, your relatives will appreciate listening to these words describing a magical place where all is pleasure and peace.

In Xanadu did Kubla Khan
A stately pleasure-dome decree:
Where Alph, the sacred river, ran
Through caverns measureless to man
    Down to a sunless sea.
So twice five miles of fertile ground
With walls and tower were girdled round:
And there were gardens bright with sinuous rills
Where blossom'd many an incense-bearing tree;
And here were forests ancient as the hills,
Enfolding sunny spots of greenery.

But O, that deep romantic chasm which slanted
Down the green hill athwart a cedarn cover!
A savage place! as holy and enchanted
As e'er beneath a waning moon was haunted
By woman wailing for her demon-lover!
And from this chasm, with ceaseless turmoil seething,
As if this earth in fast thick pants were breathing,
A mighty fountain momently was forced;

Amid whose swift half-intermitted burst
Huge fragments vaulted like rebounding hail,
Or chaffy grain beneath the thresher's flail:
And 'mid these dancing rocks at once and ever
It flung up momently the sacred river.
Five miles meandering with a mazy motion
Through wood and dale the sacred river ran,
Then reach'd the caverns measureless to man,
And sank in tumult to a lifeless ocean:
And 'mid this tumult Kubla heard from far
Ancestral voices prophesying war!

The shadow of the dome of pleasure
    Floated midway on the waves;
  Where was heard the mingled measure
    From the fountain and the caves.
It was a miracle of rare device,
A sunny pleasure-dome with caves of ice!

  A damsel with a dulcimer
    In a vision once I saw:
  It was an Abyssinian maid,
    And on her dulcimer she play'd,
  Singing of Mount Abora.
  Could I revive within me,
    Her symphony and song,
To such a deep delight 'twould win me,
That with music loud and long,
I would build that dome in air,
That sunny dome! those caves of ice!
And all who heard should see them there,
And all should cry, Beware! Beware!
His flashing eyes, his floating hair!

Weave a circle round him thrice,
  And close your eyes with holy dread,
  For he on honey-dew hath fed,
And drunk the milk of Paradise.

La Belle Dame Sans Merci

JOHN KEATS

*The next time you need extra pocket money or wish to
ingratiate yourself with the female members of the family, try
this poem. Some women (myself included) like to dream of a
wonderful knight in shining armour, and what better than to
listen to that knight's description of his ideal lady.*

"Oh, what can ail thee, knight-at arms,
  Alone and palely loitering?
The sedge has withered from the lake,
  And no birds sing.

"Oh, what can ail thee, knight-at-arms,
  So haggard and so woebegone?
The squirrel's granary is full,
  And the harvest's done.

"I see a lily on thy brow,
  With anguish moist and fever dew;
And on thy cheeks a fading rose
  Fast withereth, too,"

I met a lady in the meads,
  Full beautiful – a faëry's child;
Her hair was long, her foot was light,
  And her eyes were wild.

I made a garland for her head,
  And bracelets too, and fragrant zone;
She looked at me as she did love,
  And made sweet moan.

I set her on my pacing steed,
  And nothing else saw, all day long.
For sidelong would she bend, and sing
  A faëry's song.

She found me roots of relish sweet,
　　And honey wild, and manna dew;
And sure in language strange she said,
　　"I love thee true."

She took me to her elfin grot,
　　And there she wept, and sighed full sore;
And there I shut her wild, wild eyes
　　With kisses four.

And there she lullèd me asleep,
　　And there I dreamed, ah, woe betide!
The latest dream I ever dreamt
　　On the cold hill's side.

I saw pale kings, and princes, too,
　　Pale warriors, death-pale were they all;
They cried, "La Belle Dame Sans Merci
　　Hath thee in thrall!"

I saw their starved lips in the gloam
　　With horrid warning gapèd wide –
And I awoke, and found me here,
　　On the cold hill's side.

And this is why I sojourn here,
　　Alone and palely loitering,
Though the sedge is withered from the lake,
　　And no birds sing.

The Lady of Shalott

ALFRED, LORD TENNYSON

*This lovely poem is a paean to a beautiful woman. Camelot
itself has romantic connotations, and this expression of love is
a beautiful way to show how much you love poetry and classical
poems at that. Older relatives will appreciate your
thoughtfulness in reciting something they have heard of, and
you will enjoy the wonderful flow of words and the calmness
with which the poet has enriched the story.*

Part One

On either side the river lie
Long fields of barley and of rye,
That clothe the wold and meet the sky;
And thro' the field the road runs by
   To many-tower'd Camelot;
And up and down the people go,
Gazing where the lilies blow
Round an island there below,
   The island of Shalott.

Willows whiten, aspens quiver,
Little breezes dusk and shiver
Thro' the wave that runs for ever
By the island in the river
   Flowing down to Camelot.
Four grey walls, and four grey towers,
Overlook a space of flowers,
And the silent isle imbowers
   The Lady of Shalott.

By the margin, willow-veil'd,
Slide the heavy barges trail'd
By slow horses; and unhail'd
The shallop flitteth silken-sail'd
   Skimming down to Camelot:
But who hath seen her wave her hand?
Or at the casement seen her stand?
Or is she known in all the land,
   The Lady of Shalott?

Only reapers, reaping early
In among the bearded barley,
Hear a song that echoes cheerly
From the river winding clearly,
    Down to tower'd Camelot:
And by the moon the reaper weary,
Piling sheaves in uplands airy,
Listening, whispers "'Tis the fairy
    Lady of Shalott."

Part Two

There she weaves by night and day
A magic web with colours gay.
She has heard a whisper say,
A curse is on her if she stay
    To look down to Camelot.
She knows not what the curse may be,
And so she weaveth steadily,
And little other care hath she,
    The Lady of Shalott.

And moving thro' a mirror clear
That hangs before her all the year,
Shadows of the world appear.
There she sees the highway near
    Winding down to Camelot.
There the river eddy whirls,
And there the surly village-churls,
And the red cloaks of market girls,
    Pass onward from Shalott.

Sometimes a troop of damsels glad,
An abbot on an ambling pad,
Sometimes a curly shepherd-lad,
Or long-hair'd page in crimson clad,
    Goes by to tower'd Camelot;
And sometimes thro' the mirror blue
The knights come riding two and two:
She hath no loyal knight and true,
    The Lady of Shalott.

But in her web she still delights
To weave the mirror's magic sights,
For often thro' the silent nights
A funeral, with plumes and lights,
    And music, went to Camelot:
Or when the moon was overhead,
Came two young lovers lately wed;
"I am half sick of shadows," said
    The Lady of Shalott.

Part Three

A bow-shot from her bower-eaves,
He rode between the barley-sheaves,
The sun came dazzling thro' the leaves,
And flamed upon the brazen greaves
    Of bold Sir Lancelot.
A red-cross knight for ever kneel'd
To a lady in his shield,
That sparkled on the yellow field,
    Beside remote Shalott.

The gemmy bridle glitter'd free,
Like to some branch of stars we see
Hung in the golden Galaxy.
The bridle bells rang merrily
    As he rode down to Camelot:
And from his blazon'd baldric slung
A mighty silver bugle hung,
And as he rode his armour rung,
    Beside remote Shalott.

All in the blue unclouded weather
Thick-jewell'd shone the saddle-leather,
The helmet and the helmet-feather
Burn'd like one burning flame together,
    As he rode down to Camelot.
As often thro' the purple night,
Below the starry clusters bright,
Some bearded meteor, trailing light,
    Moves over still Shalott.

His broad clear brow in sunlight glow'd;
On burnish'd hooves his war-horse trode;
From underneath his helmet flow'd
His coal-black curls as on he rode,
    As he rode down to Camelot.
From the bank and from the river
He flash'd into the crystal mirror,
"Tirra lirra," by the river
    Sang Sir Lancelot.

She left the web, she left the loom,
She made three paces thro' the room,
She saw the water-lily bloom,
She saw the helmet and the plume,
    She look'd down to Camelot.
Out flew the web and floated wide,
The mirror crack'd from side to side;
"The curse is come upon me!" cried
    The Lady of Shalott.

Part Four

In the stormy east-wind straining,
The pale yellow woods were waning,
The broad stream in his banks complaining,
Heavily the low sky raining
 Over tower'd Camelot;
Down she came and found a boat
Beneath a willow left afloat,
And round about the prow she wrote
 The Lady of Shalott.

And down the river's dim expanse –
Like some bold seer in a trance,
Seeing all his own mischance –
With a glassy countenance
 Did she look to Camelot.
And at the closing of the day
She loosed the chain, and down she lay;
The broad stream bore her far away,
 The Lady of Shalott.

Lying, robed in snowy white
That loosely flew to left and right –
The leaves upon her falling light –
Thro' the noises of the night
 She floated down to Camelot:
And as the boat-head wound along
The willowy hills and fields among,
They heard her singing her last song,
 The Lady of Shalott.

Heard a carol, mournful, holy,
Chanted loudly, chanted lowly,
Till her blood was frozen slowly,
And her eyes were darken'd wholly,
 Turn'd to tower'd Camelot;
For ere she reach'd upon the tide
The first house by the water-side,
Singing in her song she died.
 The Lady of Shalott

Under tower and balcony,
By garden-wall and gallery,
A gleaming shape she floated by,
Dead-pale between the houses high,
    Silent into Camelot.
Out upon the wharfs they came,
Knight and burgher, lord and dame,
And round the prow they read her name,
    The Lady of Shalott.

Who is this? and what is here?
And in the lighted palace near
Died the sound of royal cheer;
And they cross'd themselves for fear,
    All the knights at Camelot:
But Lancelot mused a little space;
He said, "She has a lovely face;
God in His mercy lend her grace,
    The Lady of Shalott."

The Listeners   WALTER DE LA MARE

An eerie feeling of loneliness and unseen watchers comes
through the words of this poem. A good one for winter nights
in remote cottages when staying with grandparents. It goes
with ghost stories and strange knocks on the walls.

"Is there anybody there?" said the Traveller,
    Knocking on the moonlit door;
And his horse in the silence champed the grasses
    Of the forest's ferny floor:
And a bird flew up out of the turret,
    Above the Traveller's head:
And he smote upon the door again a second time;
    "Is there anybody there?" he said,
But no one descended to the Traveller;
    No head from the leaf-fringed sill
Leaned over and looked into his grey eyes,
    Where he stood perplexed and still.
But only a host of phantom listeners
    That dwelt in the lone house then
Stood listening in the quiet of the moonlight
    To that voice from the world of men:
Stood thronging the faint moonbeams on the dark stair,
    That goes down to the empty hall,
Hearkening in an air stirred and shaken
    By the lonely Traveller's call.
And he felt in his heart their strangeness,
    Their stillness answering his cry,
While his horse moved, cropping the dark turf,
    'Neath the starred and leafy sky;
For he suddenly smote on the door, even
    Louder, and lifted his head:
"Tell them I came, and no one answered,
    That I kept my word," he said.
Never the least stir made the listeners,
    Though every word he spake
Fell echoing through the shadowiness of the still house
    From the one man left awake:
Ay, they heard his foot upon the stirrup,
    And the sound of iron on stone,
And how the silence surged softly backward,
    When the plunging hoofs were gone.

Lord Ullin's Daughter

THOMAS CAMPBELL

A scream over the water, a wind howling through the night, a boatman determined to deliver his lord's child home. What components for a tale! This Scottish story of a fatal journey is for dark and windy nights when you can hear the howling and raging as you speak the words to your terrified younger brothers and sisters.

A chieftain to the Highlands bound
   Cries: "Boatman, do not tarry!
And I'll give thee a silver pound
   To row us o'er the ferry."

"Now, who be ye would cross Lochgyle,
   This dark and stormy water?"
"Oh, I'm the chief of Ulva's Isle,
   And this Lord Ullin's daughter.

"And fast before her father's men
   Three days we've fled together,
For should he find us in the glen
   My blood would stain the heather.

"His horsemen hard behind us ride:
   Should they our steps discover,
Then who will cheer my bonnie bride
   When they have slain her lover?"

Out spoke the hardy Highland wight,
   "I'll go, my chief, I'm ready!
It is not for your silver bright,
   But for your winsome lady.

"And by my word, the bonny bird
   In danger shall not tarry;
So, though the waves are raging white,
   I'll row you o'er the ferry."

By this the storm grew loud apace,
   The water-wraith was shrieking;
And in the scowl of heaven each face
   Grew dark as they were speaking.

But still as wilder blew the wind,
    And as the night grew drearer,
Adown the glen rode armèd men,
    Their trampling sounded nearer.

"Oh, haste thee, haste!" the lady cries,
    "Though tempests round us gather;
I'll meet the raging of the skies,
    But not an angry father."

The boat has left a stormy land,
    A stormy sea before her –
When, oh, too strong for human hand,
    The tempest gathered o'er her.

And still they rowed amidst the roar
    Of waters fast prevailing;
Lord Ullin reached that fatal shore –
    His wrath was changed to wailing:

For sore dismayed, through storm and shade,
    His child he did discover;
One lovely hand she stretched for aid,
    And one was round her lover.

"Come back! Come back!" he cried in grief
    Across the stormy water;
"And I'll forgive your Highland chief,
    My daughter – O my daughter!"

'Twas vain: the loud waves lashed the shore,
    Return or aid preventing;
The waters wild went o'er his child,
    And he was left lamenting.

O Captain! My Captain!

WALT WHITMAN

*With despair and sadness in your voice you can dramatically
render this poem of a seaman mourning the death of his
master. The four short lines at the end of each stanza need to
be rendered with suitable doom, and the last four
spaced - right - out.*

O Captain! my Captain! our fearful trip is done,
The ship has weather'd every rack, the prize we sought is won,
The port is near, the bells I hear, the people all exulting,
While follow eyes the steady keel, the vessel grim and daring;
     But O heart! heart! heart!
      O the bleeding drops of red!
       Where on the deck my Captain lies,
       Fallen cold and dead.

O Captain! my Captain! rise up and hear the bells;
Rise up - for you the flag is flung - for you the bugle trills,
For you bouquets and ribbon'd wreaths - for you the shores a-
    crowding,
For you they call, the swaying mass, their eager faces turning;
     Here, Captain! dear father!
      This arm beneath your head!
       It is some dream that on the deck
       You've fallen cold and dead.

My Captain does not answer, his lips are pale and still,
My father does not feel my arm, he has no pulse nor will;
The ship is anchor'd safe and sound, its voyage closed and done,
From fearful trip the victor ship comes in with object won;
     Exult, O shores! and sing, O bells!
      But I, with mournful tread,
       Walk the deck my Captain lies,
       Fallen cold and dead.

The Play

C. J. DENNIS

Many years ago, while I was at school, I heard this read by the illustrator who worked with the poet. It was an amazing rendition and brought out the full flavour of the wonder of a first trip to the theatre to see a Shakespearean play. Romeo and Juliet *has never been the same for me. I still see it coloured by this particular description. Try reading it aloud, and don't worry too much if you don't get the dialect quite right.*

"Wot's in a name?" she sez ... An' then she sighs,
An' clasps 'er little 'ands, an' rolls 'er eyes.
"A rose," she sez, "be any other name
Would smell the same.
Oh, w'erefore art you Romeo, young sir?
Chuck yer ole pot, an' change yer moniker!"

Doreen an' me, we bin to see a show –
The swell two-dollar touch. Bong tong, yeh know.
A chair apiece wiv velvit on the seat;
A slap-up treat.
The drarmer's writ be Shakespeare, years ago,
About a barmy goat called Romeo.

"Lady, be yonder moon I swear!" sez 'e.
An' then 'e climbs up on the balkiney;
An' there they smooge a treat, wiv pretty words
Like two love-birds.
I nudge Doreen. She whispers, "Ain't it grand!"
'Er eyes is shinin'; and I squeeze 'er 'and.

"Wot's in a name?" she sez. 'Struth, I dunno.
Billo is just as good as Romeo.
She may be Juli-er or Juli-et –
'E loves 'er yet.
If she's the tart 'e wants, then she's 'is queen,
Names never count ... But ar, I like "Doreen!".

A sweeter, dearer sound I never 'eard;
Ther's music 'angs around that little word,
Doreen! ... But wot was this I starts to say
About the play?
I'm off me beat. But when a bloke's in love
'Is thorts turns 'er way, like a 'omin' dove.

This Romeo 'e's lurkin' wiv a crew –
A dead tough crowd o' crooks – called Montague.
'Is cliner's push – wot's nicknamed Capulet –
They 'as 'em set.
Fair narks they are, jist like them back-street clicks,
Ixcep' they fights wiv skewers 'stid o' bricks.

Wot's in a name? Wot's in a string o' words?
They scraps in ole Verona wiv the'r swords,
An' never give a bloke a stray dog's chance,
An' that's Romance.
But when they deals it out wiv bricks an' boots
In Little Lon., they're low, degraded broots.

Wot's jist plain stoush wiv us, right 'ere to-day,
Is "valler" if yer fur enough away.
Some time, some writer bloke will do the trick
Wiv Ginger Mick,
Of Spadger's Lane, *'E'll* be a Romeo,
When 'e's bin dead five 'undred years or so.

Fair Juli-et, she gives 'er boy the tip.
Sez she: "Don't sling that crowd o'mine no lip;
An' if you run agin a Capulet,
Jist do a get."
'E swears 'e's done wiv lash; 'e'll chuck it clean.
(Same as I done when I first met Doreen.)

They smooge some more at that. Ar, strike me blue!
It gimme Joes to sit an' watch them two!
'E'd break away an' start to say good-bye,
An' then she'd sigh
"Ow, Ro-me-o!" an' git a strangle-holt,
An' 'ang around 'im like she feared 'e'd bolt.

Nex't day 'e words a gorspil cove about
A secret weddin'; an' they plan it out.
'E spouts a piece about 'ow 'e's bewitched:
Then they git 'itched …
Now, 'ere's the place where I fair git the pip!
She's 'is for keeps, an' yet 'e lets 'er slip!

Ar! but 'e makes me sick! A fair gazob!
'E's jist the glarsey on the soulful sob,
'E'll sigh and spruik, an' 'owl a love-sick vow –
(The silly cow!)
But when 'e's got 'er, spliced an' on the straight
'E crools the pitch, an' tries to kid it's Fate.

Aw! Fate me foot! Instid of slopin' soon
As 'e was wed, off on 'is 'oneymoon,
'Im an' 'is cobber, called Mick Curio,
They 'ave to go
An' mix it wiv that push o' Capulets
They look fer trouble; an' it's wot they gets.

A tug named Tyball (cousin to the skirt)
Sprags 'em an' makes a start to sling off dirt.
Nex' minnit there's a reel ole ding-dong go –
'Arf round or so.
Mick Curio, 'e gets it in the neck,
"Ar rats!" 'e sez, an' passes in 'is check.

Quite natchril, Romeo gits wet as 'ell.
"It's me or you!" 'e 'owls, an' wiv a yell,
Plunks Tyball through the gizzard wiv 'is sword,
'Ow I ongcored!
"Put in the boot!" I sez. "Put in the boot!"
"'Ush!" sez Doreen … "Shame!" sez some silly coot.

Then Romeo, 'e dunno wot to do.
The cops gits busy, like they allwiz do,
An' nose around until 'e gits blue funk
An' does a bunk.
They wants 'is tart to wed some other guy.
"Ah, strike!" she sez. "I wish that I could die!"

Now, this 'ere gorspil bloke's a fair shrewd 'ead.
Sez 'e "I'll dope yeh, so they'll *think* yer dead."
(I tips 'e was a cunnin' sort, wot knoo,
A thing or two.)
She takes 'is knock-out drops, up in 'er room:
They think she's snuffed, an' plant 'er in 'er tomb.

Then things gits mixed a treat an' starts to whirl.
'Ere's Romeo comes back an' finds 'is girl
Tucked in 'er little coffing, cold an' stiff,
An' in a jiff,
'E swallows lysol, throws a fancy fit,
'Ead over turkey, an' 'is soul 'as flit.

Then Juli-et wakes up an' sees 'im there,
Turns on the water-works an' tears 'er 'air,
"Dear love," she sez, "I cannot live alone!"
An' wiv a moan,
She grabs 'is pockit knife, an' ends 'er cares …
"Peanuts or lollies!" sez a boy upstairs.

The Solitary Reaper

WILLIAM WORDSWORTH

*I remember seeing, hanging on the wall in a relative's house, a
painting of a girl gathering corn in a field. On asking what it
was about, an elderly relative recited this poem. In my mind's
eye I still see the picture. It's a gentle poem, well suited to quiet
occasions in front of a fire.*

Behold her, single in the field,
   Yon solitary Highland Lass!
Reaping and singing by herself;
   Stop here, or gently pass!
Alone she cuts and binds the grain,
And sings a melancholy strain;
O listen! for the Vale profound
Is overflowing with the sound.

No Nightingale did ever chaunt
   More welcome notes to weary bands
Of travellers in some shady haunt,
   Among Arabian sands:
A voice so thrilling ne'er was heard
In spring-time from the Cuckoo-bird,
Breaking the silence of the seas
Among the farthest Hebrides.

Will no one tell me what she sings? –
   Perhaps the plaintive numbers flow
For old, unhappy, far-off things,
   And battles long ago:
Or is it some more humble lay,
Familiar matter of to-day?
Some natural sorrow, loss, or pain,
That has been, and may be again?

Whate'er the theme, the Maiden sang
   As if her song could have no ending;
I saw her singing at her work,
   And o'er the sickle bending; –
I listen'd, motionless and still;
And, as I mounted up the hill,
The music in my heart I bore,
Long after it was heard no more.

To a Skylark　　PERCY BYSSHE SHELLEY

*Australia doesn't have this particular lark, and the one it does
have doesn't sing very well, so my childhood was bereft of what
must be a very special sound. A long walk with grandparents
seems the right place for a poem such as this, which evokes
both time and place and the sounds and sights of the open air.*

Hail to thee, blithe spirit!
　Bird thou never wert,
That from heaven or near it
　Pourest thy full heart
In profuse strains of unpremeditated art.

Higher still, and higher,
　From the earth thou springest,
Like a cloud of fire;
　The blue deep thou wingest,
And singing still dost soar, and soaring ever singest.

In the golden lightning
　Of the sunken sun,
O'er which clouds are bright'ning,
　Thou dost float and run,
Like an unbodied joy whose race is just begun.

The pale purple even
　Melts around thy flight;
Like a star of Heaven,
　In the broad daylight
Thou art unseen, but yet I hear thy shrill delight.

Keen as are the arrows
　Of that silver sphere,
Whose intense lamp narrows
　In the white dawn clear,
Until we hardly see, we feel that it is there.

All the earth and air
   With thy voice is loud,
As, when night is bare,
   From one lonely cloud
The moon rains out her beams, and heaven is overflowed.

What thou art we know not;
   What is most like thee?
From rainbow clouds there flow not
   Drops so bright to see,
As from thy presence showers a rain of melody:

Like a poet hidden
   In the light of thought,
Singing hymns unbidden,
   Till the world is wrought
To sympathy with hopes and fears it heeded not:

Like a high-born maiden
   In a palace tower,
Soothing her love-laden
   Soul in secret hour
With music sweet as love, which overflows her bower:

Like a glow-worm golden,
   In a dell of dew,
Scattering unbeholden
   Its aërial hue
Among the flowers and grass which screen it from the view:

Like a rose embowered
    In its own green leaves,
By warm winds deflowered,
    Till the scent it gives
Makes faint with too much sweet those heavy-wingèd thieves:

Sound of vernal showers
    On the twinkling grass,
Rain-awakened flowers,
    All that ever was
Joyous and clear and fresh, thy music doth surpass.

Teach us, sprite or bird,
    What sweet thoughts are thine:
I have never heard
    Praise of love or wine
That panted forth a flood of rapture so divine.

Chorus hymeneal,
    Or triumphal chant,
Matched with thine would be all
    But an empty vaunt,
A thing wherein we feel there is some hidden want.

What objects are the fountains
    Of thy happy strain?
What fields, or waves, or mountains?
    What shapes of sky or plain?
What love of thine own kind? What ignorance of pain?

With thy clear, keen joyance
    Languor cannot be:
Shadow of annoyance
    Never came near thee:
Thou lovest, but ne'er knew love's sad satiety.

Waking or asleep,
    Thou of death must deem
Things more true and deep
    Than we mortals dream,
Or how could thy notes flow in such a crystal stream?

We look before and after,
    And pine for what is not:
Out sincerest laughter
    With some pain is fraught;
Our sweetest songs are those that tell of saddest thought.

Yet if we could scorn
    Hate and pride and fear,
If we were things born
    Not to shed a tear,
I know not how thy joy we ever should come near.

Better than all measures
    Of delightful sound,
Better than all treasures
    That in books are found,
Thy skill to poet were, thou scorner of the ground!

Teach me half the gladness
    That thy brain must know,
Such harmonious madness
    From my lips would flow,
The world should listen then, as I am listening now.

When the Circus Came to Town

JOHN O'BRIEN

*Near where we lived was a large piece of open land, now
covered with houses. One day a circus came and I remember
the excitement of watching them unpack, then the
disappointment when told that we would not be going.
However, I still feel that the anticipation and the watching was
perhaps better than the hot tent and the performing animals
might have been. This is nostalgia.*

When the circus came to town
With its coaches and four, and its steeds galore,
    And a band and a painted clown,
Out to the road with a shout we'd fly
To gape at the elephants trudging by,
And our hearts beat fast and our hopes ran high.
    As we followed it up and down;
For nought in the air, the sea, or sky
Could fill a spot in our youthful eye,
    When the circus came to town.

So after the show we went,
And we got in the way of the men when they
    Were rigging the circus tent,
And we knew that we stood on holy ground,
As we followed an empty van around –
And got for ourselves a belting sound,
    Which a charm to the business lent.
But we wagged it from school behind the pound,
Till some Jack Pudding our shelter found
    And word to headquarters sent.

When the circus came to town,
We swallowed hot tea with tears of glee,
    And rushed in a tumult down;
We took quite the full of our shilling's worth,
And roared at the dummy's ponderous girth,
Or yelled in a salvo of noisy mirth
    At the tricks of the painted clown.
Oh, wondrous thoughts in our minds had birth,
And we felt that the band was the best on earth,
    When the circus came to town.

We fondly recalled the scene,
Horses that pranced, and eyes entranced,
    And the smell of the kerosene;
The mule, and the monkey, and tall giraffe,
The "juggerlin'-man" with his magic staff,
The girl who went round with her photograph
    (And oh, but we thought her a queen!)
We started a show on our own behalf,
"Performed" on the back of a poddy calf,
    And sighed for the might-have-been.

Now the circus comes to town,
And it rattles along, and a bare-foot throng
    Is pacing it up and down;
And the elephants trudge as they trudged of yore,
With the shabby shebangs, and the steeds galore;
But the glee of the youngsters who shout and roar
    At the tricks of the painted clown
Is balm to my soul, and I call *encore*
To the frowsy old jokes I've heard before,
    When the circus came to town.

The Wreck of the Hesperus

HENRY WADSWORTH LONGFELLOW

*When you are feeling like declaiming to the world you couldn't
choose a better poem than this. Full of dramatic moments,
pathos, heroism and grief, it allows the full range of emotions
to be used in rendering it aloud at a special family occasion.*

It was the schooner Hesperus,
   That sailed the wintry sea;
And the skipper had taken his little daughtèr,
   To bear him company.

Blue were her eyes as the fairy flax,
   Her cheeks like the dawn of day,
And her bosom white as the hawthorn-buds,
   That ope in the month of May.

The skipper he stood beside the helm,
   His pipe was in his mouth,
And he watched how the veering flaw did blow,
   The smoke now west, now south.

Then up and spake an old sailòr,
   Had sailed the Spanish Main,
"I pray thee, put into yonder port,
   For I fear a hurricane.

"Last night, the moon had a golden ring,
   And tonight no moon we see!"
The skipper, he blew a whiff from his pipe,
   And a scornful laugh laughed he.

Colder and louder blew the wind,
   A gale from the north-east;
The snow fell hissing in the brine,
   And the billows frothed like yeast.

Down came the storm, and smote amain
   The vessel in its strength;
She shuddered and paused, like a frighted steed,
   Then leaped her cable's length.

"Come hither! come hither! my little daughtèr,
  And do not tremble so;
For I can weather the roughest gale,
  That ever wind did blow."

He wrapped her warm in his seaman's coat,
  Against the stinging blast;
He cut a rope from a broken spar,
  And bound her to the mast.

"Oh father! I hear the church-bells ring,
  O say, what may it be?"
"'Tis a fog-bell on a rock-bound coast!"
  And he steered for the open sea.

"O father! I hear the sound of guns,
  O say, what may it be?"
"Some ship in distress, that cannot live
  In such an angry sea!"

"O father! I see a gleaming light,
  O say, what may it be?"
But the father answered never a word,
  A frozen corpse was he.

Lashed to the helm, all stiff and stark,
  With his face turned to the skies,
The lantern gleamed through the gleaming snow
  On his fixed and glassy eyes.

Then the maiden clasped her hands and prayed
  That saved she might be;
And she thought of Christ who stilled the wave
  On the lake of Galilee.

And fast through the midnight dark and drear,
    Through the whistling sleet and snow,
Like a sheeted ghost, the vessel swept
    Towards the reef of Norman's Woe.

And ever the fitful gusts between
    A sound came from the land;
It was the sound of the trampling surf,
    On the rocks and the hard sea-sand.

The breakers were right beneath her bows,
    She drifted a dreary wreck,
And a whooping billow swept the crew
    Like icicles from her deck.

She struck where the white and fleecy waves
    Looked soft as carded wool,
But the cruel rocks they gored her side
    Like the horns of an angry bull.

Her rattling shrouds, all sheathed in ice,
    With the masts went by the board;
Like a vessel of glass, she stove and sank,
    Ho! ho! the breakers roared!

At day-break, on the bleak sea-beach,
    A fisherman stood aghast,
To see the form of a maiden fair,
    Lashed close to a drifting mast.

The salt sea was frozen on her breast,
    The salt tears in her eyes;
And he saw her hair, like the brown sea-weed,
    On the billows fall and rise.

Such was the wreck of the Hesperus,
    In the midnight and the snow!
Christ save us all from a death like this,
    On the reef of Norman's Woe!

For Sharing With Friends

Adventures of Isabel OGDEN NASH

*A young lady of undoubted talent is Isabel. Her adventures
would make any person jealous of her ability to outwit her
opponents. Saying this with your friends brings on a wonderful
feeling of scariness followed by relief as Isabel wins yet again.*

Isabel met an enormous bear,
Isabel, Isabel, didn't care;
The bear was hungry, the bear was ravenous,
The bear's big mouth was cruel and cavernous.
The bear said, Isabel, glad to meet you,
How do, Isabel, now I'll eat you!
Isabel, Isabel, didn't worry,
Isabel didn't scream or scurry.
She washed her hands and she straightened her hair up,
Then Isabel quietly ate the bear up.

Once in a night as black as pitch
Isabel met a wicked old witch.
The witch's face was cross and wrinkled,
The witch's gums with teeth were sprinkled,
Ho ho, Isabel! the old witch crowed,
I'll turn you into an ugly toad!
Isabel, Isabel, didn't worry,
Isabel didn't scream or scurry,
She showed no rage and she showed no rancour,
But she turned the witch into milk and drank her.

Isabel met a hideous giant,
Isabel continued self-reliant.
The giant was hairy, the giant was horrid,
He had one eye in the middle of his forehead.
Good morning Isabel, the giant said,
I'll grind your bones to make my bread.
Isabel, Isabel, didn't worry,
Isabel didn't scream or scurry.
She nibbled the zwieback that she always fed off,
And when it was gone, she cut the giant's head off.

Isabel met a troublesome doctor,
He punched and he poked till he really shocked her.
The doctor's talk was of coughs and chills
And the doctor's satchel bulged with pills.
The doctor said unto Isabel,
Swallow this, it will make you well.
Isabel, Isabel, didn't worry,
Isabel didn't scream or scurry.
She took those pills from the pill concocter,
And Isabel calmly cured the doctor.

A Bush Christening

A. B. (BANJO) PATERSON

*Don't you sometimes wish that christenings weren't such staid
occasions, and that something would happen to enliven them?
This young lad finds himself the victim of circumstance and the
bearer of a quite unusual name. Sharing this with cousins at a
christening might be a good idea.*

On the outer Barcoo where the churches are few,
   And men of religion are scanty,
On a road never cross'd 'cept by folk that are lost
   One Michael Magee had a shanty.

Now this Mike was the dad of a ten-year-old lad,
   Plump, healthy, and stoutly conditioned;
He was strong as the best, but poor Mike had no rest
   For the youngster had never been christened.

And his wife used to cry, "If the darlin' should die
   Saint Peter would not recognize him."
But by luck he survived till a preacher arrived,
   Who agreed straightaway to baptize him.

Now the artful young rogue, while they held their collogue,
   With his ear to the keyhole was listenin';
And he muttered in fright, while his features turned white,
   "What the divil and all is this christenin'?"

He was none of your dolts – he had seen them brand colts,
   And it seemed to his small understanding,
If the man in the frock made him one of the flock,
   It must mean something very like branding.

So away with a rush he set off for the bush,
   While the tears in his eyelids they glistened –
"'Tis outrageous," says he, "to brand youngsters like me;
   I'll be dashed if I'll stop to be christened!"

Like a young native dog he ran into a log,
  And his father with language uncivil,
Never heeding the "praste", cried aloud in his haste
  "Come out and be christened, you divil!"

But he lay there as snug as a bug in a rug,
  And his parents in vain might reprove him,
Till his reverence spoke (he was fond of a joke)
  "I've a notion," says he, "that'll move him.

"Poke a stick up the log, give the spalpeen a prog;
  Poke him aisy – don't hurt him or maim him;
'Tis not long that he'll stand, I've the water at hand,
  As he rushes out this end I'll name him.

"Here he comes, and for shame! ye've forgotten the name –
  Is it Patsy or Michael or Dinnis?"
Here the youngster ran out, and the priest gave a shout –
  'Take your chance, anyhow, wid 'Maginnis!' "

As the howling young cub ran away to the scrub
  Where he knew that pursuit would be risky,
The priest, as he fled, flung a flask at his head
  That was labelled "Maginnis's Whisky"!

Now Maginnis Magee has been made a J.P.,
  And the one thing he hates more than sin is
To be asked by the folk, who have heard of the joke,
  How he came to be christened Maginnis!

Catalogue

ROSALIE MOORE

*Anyone who has been owned by a cat will understand this
poem. Try reading it with a cat on your lap, or in the garden
with your friends and the cat stretched out together on the
grass. I bet the cat takes up more space than you do.*

Cats sleep fat and walk thin.
Cats, when they sleep, slump;
When they wake, stretch and begin
Over, pulling their ribs in.
Cats walk thin.

Cats wait in a lump,
Jump in a streak.
Cats, when they jump, are sleek
As a grape slipping its skin –
They have technique.
Oh, cats don't creak.
They sneak.

Cats sleep fat.
They spread out comfort underneath them
Like a good mat,
As if they picked the place
And then sat.
You walk around one
As if he were the city hall
After that.

If male,
A cat is apt to sing on a major scale;
This concert is for everybody, this
Is wholesale.
For a baton, he wields a tail.

(He is also found,
When happy, to resound
With an enclosed and private sound.)

A cat condenses.
He pulls in his tail to go under bridges,
And himself to go under fences.
Cats fit
In any size box or kit;
And if a large pumpkin grew under one,
He could arch over it.

When everyone else is just ready to go out,
The cat is just ready to come in.
He's not where he's been.
Cats sleep fat and walk thin.

Colonel Fazackerley

CHARLES CAUSLEY

*What a wonderful name to have, perfect for confronting a
ghost! This poem should be said at impromptu concerts or as
part of an evening's entertainment when staying overnight
with a friend.*

Colonel Fazackerley Butterworth-Toast
Bought an old castle complete with a ghost,
But someone or other forgot to declare
To Colonel Fazack that the spectre was there.

On the very first evening, while waiting to dine,
The Colonel was taking a fine sherry wine,
When the ghost, with a furious flash and a flare,
Shot out of the chimney and shivered, "Beware!"

Colonel Fazackerley put down his glass
And said,"My dear fellow, that's really first class!
I just can't conceive how you do it at all.
I imagine you're going to a Fancy Dress Ball?"

At this, the dread ghost gave a withering cry.
Said the Colonel (his monocle firm in his eye),
"Now just how you do it I wish I could think.
Do sit down and tell me, and please have a drink."

The ghost in his phosphorous cloak gave a roar
And floated about between ceiling and floor.
He walked through a wall and returned through a pane
And backed up the chimney and came down again.

Said the Colonel, "With laughter I'm feeling quite weak!"
(As trickles of merriment ran down his cheek).
"My house-warming party I hope you won't spurn.
You *must* say you'll come and you'll give us a turn!"

At this, the poor spectre – quite out of his wits –
Proceeded to shake himself almost to bits.
He rattled his chains and he clattered his bones
And he filled the whole castle with mumbles and moans.

But Colonel Fazackerley, just as before,
Was simply delighted and called out, "Encore!"
At which the ghost vanished, his efforts in vain,
And never was seen at the castle again.

"Oh dear, what a pity!" said Colonel Fazack.
"I don't know his name, so I can't call him back."
And then with a smile that was hard to define,
Colonel Fazackerley went in to dine.

David and Goliath ANONYMOUS

*Tranthlate all the eth'th and you'll work out that thith ith the
Bible thtory of the day a giant wath beaten by a thmall boy.*

Goliath of Gath
With helmet of brath
Wath theated one day
Upon the green grath.

When up thkipped thlim David
A thervant of Thaul,
And thaid I will thmite thee
Although I am thmall.

Thlim David thkipped down
To the edge of the thtream,
And from it'th thmooth thurface
Five thmooth thtoneth he took,

He thkilfully thlung one –
It thped through the thky,
And hit that old thinner
Right over the eye.

Goliath fell down
In a thwoon on the thward,
Thlim David thkipped up,
And drew out hith thword.

He loothened hith corthetth
And thevered hith head,
And all Ithrael thouted –
"Yippee! Goliath ith dead!"

Griselda

ELEANOR FARJEON

*At some time we have all been guilty of raiding the fridge and
the cupboards, of taking a cake we know is being saved, of
eating the last chocolate or the last of the cheese. I think this
poem would be best after a midnight feast at a friend's house
when you don't have to take the blame for the mess on the
floor of the bedroom.*

Griselda is greedy, I'm sorry to say.
She isn't contented with four meals a day,
Like breakfast and dinner and supper and tea
(I've had to put tea after supper – you see
    Why, don't you?)
Griselda is greedy as greedy can be.

She snoops about the larder
For sundry small supplies,
She breaks the little crusty bits
Off rims of apple pies,
She pokes the roast-potato-dish
When Sunday dinner's done,
And if there are two left in it
Griselda snitches one:
Cold chicken and cold cauliflower
She pulls in little chunks –
And when Cook calls:
    "What *are* you doing there?"
    Griselda bunks.

Griselda is greedy. Well, that's how she feels,
She simply can't help eating in-between meals,
And always forgets what it's leading to, though
The Doctor has frequently told her: "You know
    Why, *don't* you?"
When the stomach-ache starts and Griselda says:
    "Oh!"

She slips down to the dining-room
When everyone's in bed,
For cheese-rind on the supper-tray,
And buttered crusts of bread,
A biscuit from the biscuit-box,
Lump sugar from the bowl,
A gherkin from the pickle-jar,
Are all Griselda's toll;
    She tastes the salted almonds,
    And she tries the candied fruits –
And when Dad shouts:
    "Who *is* it down below?"
    Griselda scoots.

Criselda is greedy. Her relatives scold,
And tell her how sorry she'll be when she's old,
She will lose her complexion, she's sure to grow fat,
She will spoil her inside – does she know what she's at? –
    (Why *do* they?)
Some people *are* greedy. Leave it at that.

I had a Hippopotamus

PATRICK BARRINGTON

*What a wonderful pet to have around the house, and what
amazing rhymes the poet manages to contrive. Half the joy of
this poem is saying the words which start "hippo-" and end
something else. Great to read out loud; a pity it has a sad
ending.*

I had a hippopotamus; I kept him in a shed
And fed him upon vitamins and vegetable bread;
I made him my companion on many cheery walks
And had his portrait done by a celebrity in chalks.

His charming eccentricities were known on every side,
The creature's popularity was wonderfully wide;
He frolicked with the Rector in a dozen friendly tussles,
Who could not but remark upon his hippopotamuscles.

If he should be afflicted by depression or the dumps,
By hippopotameasles or the hippopotamumps,
I never knew a particle of peace till it was plain
He was hippopotamasticating properly again.

I had a hippopotamus; I loved him as a friend;
But beautiful relationships are bound to have an end.
Time takes, alas! our joys from us and robs us of our blisses;
My hippopotamus turned out a hippopotamissis.

My housekeeper regarded him with jaundice in her eye;
She did not want a colony of hippopotami;
She borrowed a machine-gun from her soldier-nephew, Percy,
And showed my hippopotamus no hippopotamercy.

My house now lacks the glamour that the charming creature
    gave,
The garage where I kept him is as silent as the grave;
No longer he displays among the motor-tyres and spanners
His hippopotamastery of hippopotamanners.

No longer now he gambols in the orchard in the Spring
No longer do I lead him through the village on a string;
No longer in the mornings does the neighbourhood rejoice
To his hippopotamusically-modulated voice.

I had a hippopotamus; but nothing upon earth
Is constant in its happiness or lasting in its mirth.
No joy that life can give me can be strong enough to smother
My sorrow for that might-have-been-a-hippopotamother.

The Jumblies

EDWARD LEAR

*The wonderful fantasy of this impossible journey is best shared
out loud with friends who understand about fun and enjoy
magical words and imaginative use of language.*

The went to sea in a Sieve, they did,
    In a Sieve they went to sea;
In spite of all their friends could say,
On a winter's morn, on a stormy day,
    In a Sieve they went to sea!
And when the Sieve turned round and round
And everyone cried, "You'll all be drowned!"
They cried aloud, "Our Sieve ain't big,
But we don't care a button, we don't care a fig!
    In a Sieve we'll go to sea!"
Far and few, far and few,
Are the lands where the Jumblies live;
Their heads are green and their hands are blue,
    And they went to sea in a Sieve.

They sailed away in a Sieve, they did,
    In a Sieve they sailed so fast,
With only a beautiful pea-green veil
Tied with a riband, by way of a sail,
    To a small tobacco-pipe mast:
And everyone said who saw them go,
"Oh, won't they be soon upset, you know!
For the sky is dark, and the voyage is long,
And happen what may, it's extremely wrong
    In a Sieve to sail so fast!"

The water it soon came in, it did,
    The water it soon came in;
So to keep them dry they wrapped their feet
In a pinky paper all folded neat,
    And they fastened it down with a pin.
And they passed the night in a crockery jar,
And each of them said, "How wise we are!
Though the sky be dark, and the voyage be long,
Yet we never can think we were rash or wrong
    While round in our Sieve we spin!"

And all night long they sailed away;
    And when the sun went down
They whistled and warbled a moony song,
The echoing sound of a coppery gong.
    In the shade of the mountains brown.
"O Timballo! How happy we are
When we live in a Sieve and a crockery jar,
And all night long in the moonlight pale
We sail away with a pea-green veil
    In the shade of the mountains brown!"

They sailed to the Western Sea, they did,
    To a land all covered with trees,
And they bought an Owl, and a useful Cart,
And a pound of Rice, and a Cranberry Tart,
    And a hive of Silvery Bees.
And they bought a Pig, and some green Jackdaws,
And a lovely Monkey with lollipop paws,
And forty bottles of Ring-Bo-Ree,
    And no end of Stilton Cheese.

And in twenty years they all came back,
    In twenty years or more,
And everyone said, "How tall they've grown!"
For they've been to the Lakes, and the Torrible Zone,
    And the hills of the Chankly Bore!"
And they drank their health, and gave them a feast
Of dumplings made of beautiful yeast;
And everyone said, "If we only live,
We, too, will go to sea in a Sieve –
    To the hills of the Chankly Bore!"
Far and few, far and few,
    Are the lands where the Jumblies live;
Their heads are green and their hands are blue,
    And they went to sea in a Sieve.

The Lion and Albert

MARRIOTT EDGAR

This must be read with a pseudo-northern accent. If you start saying this aloud in the presence of adults, be warned, they will join in. Better to keep it for your friends. A sad tale of a boy, a stick and a lion, and that's only half of it.

There's a famous seaside place called Blackpool,
　That's noted for fresh air and fun,
And Mr and Mrs Ramsbottom
　Went there with young Albert, their son.

A grand little lad were young Albert,
　All dressed in his best; quite a swell
With a stick with an 'orse's 'ead 'andle,
　The finest that Woolworth's could sell.

They didn't think much to the Ocean:
　The waves, they was fiddlin' and small,
There was no wrecks and nobody drownded,
　Fact nothing to laugh at at all.

So, seeking for further amusement,
　They paid and went into the Zoo,
Where they'd Lions and Tigers and Camels,
　And old ale and sandwiches too.

There were one great big Lion called Wallace;
　His nose was all covered with scars –
He lay in a somnolent posture
　With the side of his face on the bars.

Now Albert had heard about Lions,
　How they was ferocious and wild –
To see Wallace lying so peaceful,
　Well, it didn't seem right to the child.

So straightway the brave little feller,
    Not showing a morsel of fear,
Took his stick with the 'orse's 'ead 'andle
    And pushed it in Wallace's ear.

You could see that the Lion didn't like it,
    For giving a kind of a roll,
He pulled Albert inside the cage, with 'im,
    And swallowed the little lad 'ole.

Then Pa, who had seen the occurrence,
    And didn't know what to do next,
Said, "Mother! Yon Lion's ate Albert,"
    And Mother said, "Eee, I am vexed!"

The keeper was quite nice about it;
    He said, "What a nasty mishap.
Are you sure it's *your* boy he's eaten?"
    Pa said, "Am I sure? There's his cap!"

The manager had to be sent for.
    He came and said, "What's to do?"
Pa said, "Yon Lion's ate Albert,
    And 'im in his Sunday clothes, too."

Then Mother said, "Right's right, young feller;
    I think it's a shame and a sin
For a lion to go and eat Albert,
    And after we've paid to come in."

The manager wanted no trouble,
    He took out his purse right away,
Saying, "How much to settle this matter?"
    And Pa said, "What do you usually pay?"

But Mother had turned a bit awkward
    When she thought where her Albert had gone.
She said, "No! Someone's got to be summonsed," –
    So that was decided upon.

Then off they went to the P'lice Station,
    In front of the magistrate chap;
They told 'im what happened to Albert,
    And proved it by showing his cap.

The Magistrate gave his opinion
    That no-one was really to blame
And he said that he hoped the Ramsbottoms
    Would have further sons to their name.

At that Mother got proper blazing,
    "And thank you, sir, kindly," said she.
"What, waste all our lives raising children
    To feed ruddy Lions? Not me!"

Mr Nobody

ANONYMOUS

Under the floor, inside cupboards, hiding in the outhouse is the person who does all the things you didn't do. If you are in trouble, or your friend has temporarily left home as a result of letting out the goldfish, this is the poem to share. You know it wasn't your fault, and now you have someone to blame.

I know a funny little man,
    As quiet as a mouse.
He does the mischief that is done
    In everybody's house.
Though no one ever sees his face,
    Yet one and all agree
That every plate we break, was cracked
    By Mr Nobody.

'Tis he who always tears our books,
    Who leaves the door ajar.
He picks the buttons from our shirts,
    And scatters pins afar.
That squeaking door will always squeak –
    For prithee, don't you see?
We leave the oiling to be done
    By Mr Nobody.

He puts damp wood upon the fire,
    That kettles will not boil:
His are the feet that bring in mud
    And all the carpets soil.
The papers that so oft are lost –
    Who had them last but he?
There's no one tosses them about
    But Mr Nobody.

The fingermarks upon the door
    By none of us were made.
We never leave the blinds unclosed
    To let the curtains fade.
The ink we never spill! The boots
    That lying round you see,
Are not our boots – they all belong
    To Mr Nobody.

My Shadow   ROBERT LOUIS STEVENSON

*Do you remember the first time you realized you had a
shadow? And do you remember how you chased it, jumped on
it, tried to run away? Yet it stuck to you? Share this with a
small friend who has just discovered a shadow, or recite it
while the dog or cat chases aimlessly in circles.*

I have a little shadow that goes in and out with me,
And what can be the use of him is more than I can see.
He is very, very like me from the heels up to the head;
And I see him jump before me when I jump into my bed.

The funniest thing about him is the way he likes to grow –
Not at all like proper children, which is always very slow;
For he sometimes shoots up taller, like an india-rubber ball,
And he sometimes gets so little that there's none of him at all.

He hasn't got a notion of how children ought to play,
And can only make a fool of me in every sort of way.
He stays so close beside me he's a coward you can see;
I'd think shame to stick to nursie as that shadow sticks to me.

One morning very early, before the sun was up,
I rose and found the shining dew on every buttercup;
But my lazy little shadow, like an arrant sleepy-head,
Had stayed at home behind me, and was fast asleep in bed.

Oh, I Wish I'd Looked After Me Teeth

PAM AYRES

A young friend of mine introduced me to this poem in a moment of morose thought as he contemplated a trip to the dentist. It's a poem to share with a friend after removal of a tooth, the installation of ironmongery, or a horrible filling. You can sit and commiserate with each other.

Oh, I wish I'd looked after me teeth,
   And spotted the perils beneath,
All the toffees I chewed,
   And the sweet sticky food,
Oh, I wish I'd looked after me teeth.

I wish I'd been that much more willin'
   When I had more tooth there than fillin'
To pass up gobstoppers,
   From respect to me choppers,
And to buy something else with me shillin'.

When I think of the lollies I licked,
   And the liquorice allsorts I picked,
Sherbet dabs, big and little,
   All that hard peanut brittle,
My conscience gets horribly pricked.

My mother, she told me no end,
   "If you got a tooth, you got a friend."
I was young then, and careless,
   My toothbrush was hairless,
I never had much time to spend.

Oh I showed them the toothpaste all right,
   I flashed it about late at night,
But up-and-down brushin'
And pokin' and fussin'
   Didn't seem worth the time – I could bite!

If I'd known I was paving the way
   To cavities, caps and decay,
The murder of fillin's
   Injections and drillin's,
I'd have thrown all me sherbet away.

So I lay in the old dentist's chair,
   And I gaze up his nose in despair,
And his drill it do whine,
   In these molars of mine.
"Two amalgam," he'll say, "for in there."

How I laughed at my mother's false teeth,
   As they foamed in the waters beneath.
But now comes the reckonin'
   It's *me* they are beckonin'
Oh, I *wish* I'd looked after me teeth.

Platypus and Kookaburra

REX INGAMELLS

The grass is always greener on the other side of the fence, so grownups tell us. Here are two unique beasts who find out wishes don't always come true. A friend feeling let down or wishing for something not possible might appreciate being introduced to this bird and beast.

Platypus and Kookaburra
sat on a stump of gum,
watching streaks of sunset glide
and hearing insects hum.
The streaks were blue and red and green;
the insects had a yellow sheen.

Said Platypus, "If I but knew
the way to fly, I'd be
a Platyburrakookapus
and live up in a tree."
Said Kookaburra, "I'll be blowed;
the river-bank has overflowed.

"My feet," he said, "are getting wet;
the water's touching us.
O, how I wish that I could be
a Kookaplatyburrapus
so I could safely splash and scud
through pools of deep and gorgeous mud."

Upon that instant Bunyip came
and said, "Your will be done:
you'll both be what you want to be
by rising of the sun."
At that the streaks of blue and red
were gone and stars were there instead.

The morning came, as mornings do;
but what a morning that!
A Platyburrakookapus,
with beak as flat as flat,
crouched on a gum-branch high aloft:
and when he tried to laugh he coughed.

And, flopping in the mud and water
of the riverside,
a Kookaplatyburrapus
tried and tried and tried,
but tried in vain, to show that he
was clever – for he couldn't be.

That night the Bunyip came and climbed
the highest gumtree limb,
and Platyburrakookapus
was soon inside of him:
and then he ate without a fuss
poor Kookaplatyburrapus.

Sir Smasham Uppe

E. V. RIEU

*Afternoon tea with a friend! What a delightful idea, except that
I don't know that I want to have tea with this friend. This is a
good poem to perform with actions so that you and your
friends can enjoy the smashing time together.*

Good afternoon, Sir Smasham Uppe!
We're having tea: do take a cup!
Sugar and milk? Now let me see –
Two lumps, I think: ... Good gracious me!
The silly thing slipped off your knee!
Pray don't apologize, old chap:
A very trivial mishap!
So clumsy of you? How absurd!
My dear Sir Smasham, not a word!
Now do sit down and have another,
And tell us all about your brother –
You know, the one who broke his head.
Is the poor fellow still in bed? –
A chair – allow me, sir! ... Great Scott!
That *was* a nasty smash! Eh, what?
Oh, not at all: the chair was old –
Queen Anne, or so we have been told.
We've got at least a dozen more:
Just leave the pieces on the floor.
I want you to admire our view:
Come nearer to the window, do;
And look how beautiful ... Tut, tut!
You didn't see that it was shut?
I hope you are not badly cut!
Not hurt? A fortunate escape!
Amazing! Not a single scrape!
And now, if you have finished tea,
I fancy you might like to see
A little thing or two I've got.
That china plate? Yes, worth a lot:
A beauty too ... Ah, there it goes!
I trust it didn't hurt your toes?
Your elbow brushed it off the shelf?
Of course: I've done the same myself.
And now, my dear Sir Smasham – Oh,
You surely don't intend to go?
You *must* be off? Well, come again.
So glad you're fond of porcelain!

Three Jolly Huntsmen

ANONYMOUS

Anonymous has written some good verse, and this is one of them. Another to share aloud with friends taking the various parts. I wonder if they found anything while hunting on St. George's Day?

Three jolly huntsmen,
I've heard people say,
Went hunting together
On St. David's Day.

All day they hunted,
And nothing could they find,
But a ship a-sailing,
A-sailing with the wind.

One said it was a ship,
The other he said, Nay;
The third said it was a house,
With the chimney blown away.

And all the night they hunted,
And nothing could they find
But the moon a-gliding,
A-gliding with the wind.

One said it was the moon,
The other he said, Nay;
The third said it was a cheese,
And half of it cut away.

And all the day they hunted,
And nothing did they find
But a hedgehog in a bramble-bush,
And that they left behind.

The first said it was a hedgehog,
The second he said, Nay;
The third said it was a pin cushion,
And the pins stuck in wrong way.

And all the night they hunted,
And nothing could they find
But a hare in a turnip-field,
And that they left behind.

The first said it was a hare,
The second he said, Nay;
The third said it was a calf,
And the cow had run away.

And all the day they hunted,
And nothing could they find
But an owl in a holly-tree,
And that they left behind.

One said it was an owl,
The second he said, Nay;
The third said 'twas an old man,
And his beard was growing gray.

The Triantiwontigongolope

C. J. DENNIS

*An imaginary insect (I think) which lives in Australia and has
an almost unpronounceable name. However, if you say the poem
with friends, you'll find the poet helps you with pronunciation
in the last few lines of each stanza.*

There's a very funny insect that you do not often spy,
And it isn't quite a spider, and it isn't quite a fly;
It is something like a beetle, and a little like a bee,
But nothing like a woolly grub that climbs upon a tree.
Its name is quite a hard one, but you'll learn it soon, I hope,
So, try:
   Tri –
     Tri – anti – wonti –
       Triantiwontigongolope.

It lives on weeds and wattle-gum, and has a funny face;
Its appetite is hearty, and its manners a disgrace.
When first you come upon it, it will give you quite a scare,
But when you look for it again you find it isn't there.
And unless you call it softly it will stay away and mope.
So, try:
   Tri –
     Tri – anti – wonti –
       Triantiwontigongolope.

It trembles if you tickle it or tread upon its toes;
It is not an early riser, but it has a snubbish nose.
If you sneer at it, or scold it, it will scuttle off in shame,
But it purrs and purrs quite proudly if you call it by its name,
And offer it some sandwiches of sealing-wax and soap.
So, try:
    Tri –
        Tri – anti – wonti –
            Triantiwontigongolope.

But of course you haven't seen it; and I truthfully confess
That I haven't seen it either, and I don't know its address.
For there isn't such an insect, though there really might have been
If the trees and grass were purple, and the sky was bottle-green.
It's just a little joke of mine, which you'll forgive, I hope.
Oh, try:
    Try!
        Tri – anti – wonti –
            Triantiwontigongolope.

Who Can Remember Emily Frying?

ROGER McGOUGH

*Only Roger McGough could write such a play on words and
language use. It does set you thinking about ordinary
inventions. Perhaps with the help of friends you can write
more verses about the person who invented pizza or
hamburgers or something else that tickles your fancy. I can't
remember Emily Frying, can you?*

The Grand Old Duke of Wellington
Gave us the wellington boot.
The Earl of Sandwich, so they say,
Invented the sandwich. The suit

Blues saxophonists choose to wear
Is called after Zoot Sims (a Zoot suit).
And the inventor of the saxophone?
Mr Sax, of course. (Toot! Toot!)

And we all recall, no trouble at all,
That buccaneer, long since gone,
Famed for his one-legged underpants –
"Why, shiver me timbers" – Long John.

But who can remember Emily Frying?
(Forgotten, not being a man.)
For she it was who invented
The household frying pan.

And what about Hilary Teapot?
And her cousin, Charlotte Garden-Hose?
Who invented things to go inside birdcages
(You know, for budgies to swing on). Those.

For Thoughtful Occasions

All the World's a Stage

WILLIAM SHAKESPEARE
From *As You Like It*, Act 2 Scene 7

*This is sometimes called the Seven Ages of Man, as it details
the life of a man from birth to death. It's worth thinking about
the stereotypes evident even in Shakespeare's time – whining
school boys, jealous young men, senile old men. Nothing
changes; the world and mankind go on making the same
mistakes in each age.*

All the world's a stage,
And all the men and women merely players:
They have their exits and their entrances;
And one man in his time plays many parts,
His acts being seven ages. At first the infant,
Mewling and puking in the nurse's arms.
And then the whining schoolboy, with his satchel,
And shining morning face, creeping like snail
Unwillingly to school. And then the lover,
Sighing like furnace, with a woeful ballad
Made to his mistress' eyebrow. Then a soldier,
Full of strange oaths, and bearded like the pard,
Jealous in honour, sudden and quick in quarrel,
Seeking the bubble reputation
Even in the cannon's mouth. And then the justice,
In fair round belly with good capon lin'd,
With eyes severe, and beard of formal cut.
Full of wise saws and modern instances;
And so he plays his part. The sixth age shifts
Into the lean and slipper'd pantaloon,
With spectacles on nose and pouch on side,
His youthful hose well sav'd, a world too wide
For his shrunk shank; and his big manly voice,
Turning again toward childish treble, pipes
And whistles in his sound. Last scene of all,
That ends this strange eventful history,
Is second childishness and mere oblivion,
Sans teeth, sans eyes, sans taste, sans everything.

Bagpipe Music

LOUIS MACNEICE

*This is difficult to read but worth the effort involved. It's a sad
indictment of life when unemployment is rife and the hope of
sufficient food, a job and a home have become an unreal dream.
Between the lines of despair the humour comes through in the
words and the rhythm.*

It's no go the merrygoround, it's no go the rickshaw,
All we want is a limousine and a ticket for the peepshow.
Their knickers are made of crêpe-de-chine, their shoes are made
       of python,
Their halls are lined with tiger rugs and their walls with heads of
       bison.

John MacDonald found a corpse, put it under the sofa,
Waited till it came to life and hit it with a poker,
Sold its eyes for souvenirs, sold its blood for whiskey,
Kept its bones for dumbbells to use when he was fifty.

It's no go the Yogi-man, it's no go Blavatsky,
All we want is a bank balance and a bit of skirt in a taxi.

Annie MacDougall went to milk, caught her foot in the heather,
Woke to hear a dance record playing of Old Vienna.
It's no go your maidenheads, it's no go your culture,
All we want is a Dunlop tyre and the devil mend the puncture.

The Laird o' Phelps spent Hogmanay declaring he was sober,
Counted his feet to prove the fact and found he had one foot
       over.
Mrs. Carmichael had her fifth, looked at the job with repulsion,
Said to the midwife "Take it away; I'm through with
       overproduction."

It's no go the gossip column, it's no go the Ceilidh,
All we want is a mother's help and a sugar-stick for the baby.

Willie Murray cut his thumb, couldn't count the damage,
Took the hide of an Ayrshire cow and used it for a bandage.
His brother caught three hundred cran when the seas were
      lavish,
Threw the bleeders back in the sea and went upon the parish.

It's no go the Herring Board, it's no go the Bible,
All we want is a packet of fags when our hands are idle.

It's no go the picture palace, it's no go the stadium,
It's no go the country cot with a pot of pink geraniums,
It's no go the Government grants, it's no go the elections,
Sit on your arse for fifty years and hang your hat on a pension.

It's no go my honey love, it's no go my poppet;
Work your hands from day to day, the winds will blow the profit.
The glass is falling hour by hour, the glass will fall forever,
But if you break the bloody glass you won't hold up the weather.

The Bargain

SIR PHILIP SIDNEY

*Persevere with the English, a translation into today's speech
makes it a different poem. Love poetry which is
straightforward and accessible to young people is hard to find.
A friend would surely like this one.*

My true loue hath my hart, and I haue his,
By iust exchange, one for another giu'ne.
I hold his deare, and myne he cannot misse:
There neuer was a better bargaine driu'ne.

His hart in me, keepes me and him in one,
My hart in him, his thoughts and senses guides:
He loues my hart, for once it was his owne:
I cherish his because in me it bides.

His hart his wound receiued from my sight:
My hart was wounded, with his wounded hart,
For as from me, on him his hurt did light,
So still me thought in me his hurt did smart:

Both equall hurt, in this change sought our blisse:
My true loue hath my hart and I haue his.

Because I Could Not Stop for Death

EMILY DICKINSON

*Here is a poet who writes words in a way not acceptable in
English language classes. They don't scan, capital letters are
scattered everywhere, yet the whole is a poem profound in its
meaning, giving something new every time it is read.*

Because I could not stop for Death –
He kindly stopped for me –
The Carriage held but just Ourselves –
And Immortality.

We slowly drove – He knew no haste
And I had put away
My labour and my leisure too,
For His Civility –

We passed the School, where Children strove
At Recess – in the Ring –
We passed the Fields of Gazing Grain –
We passed the Setting Sun –

Or rather – He passed Us –
The Dews drew quivering and chill –
For only Gossamer, my Gown –
My Tippet – only Tulle –

We paused before a House that seemed
A Swelling of the Ground –
The Roof was scarcely visible –
The Cornice – in the Ground –

Since then – 'tis Centuries – and yet
Feels shorter than the Day
I first surmised the Horses Heads
Were toward Eternity –

Big and Little Things

ALFRED H. MILES

*We all need to understand our limitations, especially in the
frustrating years before we are legally adult. I think every
person reading this will find some comfort in things they can
do and will cease to worry about the things they cannot do
because of age, experience or skill.*

I cannot do the big things
   That I should like to do,
To make the earth for ever fair,
   The sky for ever blue.

But I can do the small things
   That help to make it sweet,
Though clouds arise and fill the skies,
   And tempests beat.

I cannot stay the raindrops
   That tumble from the skies;
But I can wipe the tears away
   From baby's pretty eyes.

I cannot make the sun shine,
   Or warm the winter bleak;
But I can make the summer come
   On sister's rosy cheek.

I cannot stay the storm clouds,
   Or drive them from their place;
But I can clear the clouds away
   From brother's troubled face.

I cannot make the corn grow,
    Or work upon the land;
But I can put new strength and will
    In father's busy hand.

I cannot stay the east wind,
    Or thaw its icy smart;
But I can keep a corner warm
    In mother's loving heart.

I cannot do the big things
    That I should like to do,
To make the earth for ever fair,
    The sky for ever blue.

But I can do the small things
    That help to make it sweet,
Though clouds arise and fill the skies
    And tempests beat.

Death

JOHN DONNE

*Not something we want to talk about, but at some time we
must ponder on our own mortality. This seventeenth-century
writing shows us that death is not something to be afraid of,
but more a reward for life, as death itself shall die to give
eternal life to those who believe in the hereafter.*

Death, be not proud, though some have called thee
Mighty and dreadful, for thou art not so;
For those whom thou thinkest thou dost overthrow
Die not, poor Death; nor yet canst thou kill me.
From Rest and Sleep, which but thy picture be,
Much pleasure, then from thee much more must flow,
And soonest our best men with thee do go –
Rest of their bones and souls' delivery!
Thou'rt slave to fate, chance, kings, and desperate men,
And dost with poison, war and sickness dwell;
And poppy or charms can make us sleep as well
And better than thy stroke. Why swell'st thou, then?
One short sleep past, we wake eternally,
And Death shall be no more. Death, thou shalt die!

Do Not Go Gentle Into That Good Night

DYLAN THOMAS

Poets give us the chance to reflect on topics we might normally shun because of discomfort or embarrassment. Here we are faced with the end of life, not a gentle end of acceptance, but a raging against the frustration of reaching our appointed life span. Different from the approach of John Donne, but valid in its own belief that acceptance of mortality is the beginning of understanding death of spirit and body.

Do not go gentle into that good night,
Old age should burn and rave at close of day;
Rage, rage against the dying of the light.

Though wise men at their end know dark is right,
Because their words had forked no lightning they
Do not go gentle into that good night.

Good men, the last wave by, crying how bright
Their frail deeds might have danced in a green bay,
Rage, rage against the dying of the light.

Wild men who caught and sang the sun in flight,
And learn, too late, they grieved it on its way,
Do not go gentle into that good night.

Grave men, near death, who see with blinding sight
Blind eyes could blaze like meteors and be gay,
Rage, rage against the dying of the light.

And you, my father, there on the sad height,
Curse, bless, me now with your fierce tears, I pray.
Do not go gentle into that good night.
Rage, rage against the dying of the light.

The Donkey

G. K. CHESTERTON

*The Bible tells us that an ass carried Christ into Jerusalem, and
an ass carried his Mother to Bethlehem that first Christmas.
Legend tells us that this is why the ass bears a cross on his
shoulders. Here the ass has his say in a short emotional
outburst of remembered injustice.*

When fishes flew and forests walked
   And figs grew upon thorn,
Some moment when the moon was blood,
   Then surely I was born.

With monstrous head and sickening cry
   And ears like errant wings,
The devil's walking parody
   On all four-footed things.

The tattered outlaw of the earth,
   Of ancient crooked will;
Starve, scourge, deride me: I am dumb,
   I keep my secret still.

Fools! For I also had my hour;
   One far fierce hour and sweet:
There was a shout about my ears,
   And palms before my feet.

Harvest Hymn

JOHN BETJEMAN

Read this carefully. The words are not those of the school hymn book, but a parody showing the damage agricultural methods are inflicting on our environment. There might be humour in the words, but there is also a lot of truth.

We spray the fields and scatter
The poison on the ground
So that no wicked wild flowers
Upon our farm be found.
We like whatever helps us
To line our purse with pence;
The twenty-four-hour broiler-house
And neat electric fence.

All concrete sheds around us
And Jaguars in the yard,
The telly lounge and deep-freeze
Are ours from working hard.

We fire the fields for harvest,
The hedges swell the flame,
The oak trees and the cottages
From which our fathers came.
We give no compensation,
The earth is ours today,
And if we lose on arable,
Then bungalows will pay.

All concrete sheds … etc.

Home Thoughts From Abroad

ROBERT BROWNING

*Having lived in three countries, and visited others, I know that
an English spring is a special time. Flowers after the cold
winter, birds singing and building nests; the whole world seems
to celebrate the release from winter.*

Oh, to be in England
Now that April's there,
And whoever wakes in England
Sees, some morning, unaware,
That the lowest boughs and the brushwood sheaf
Round the elm-tree bole are in tiny leaf,
While the chaffinch sings on the orchard bough
In England – now!
And after April, when May follows,
And the whitethroat builds, and all the swallows!
Hark, where my blossomed pear tree in the hedge
Leans to the field and scatters on the clover
Blossoms and dewdrops – at the bent spray's edge –
That's the wise thrush; he sings each song twice over
Lest you should think he never could recapture
The first fine careless rapture!
And, though the fields look rough with hoary dew,
All will be gay when noontide wakes anew
The buttercups, the little children's dower,
Far brighter than this gaudy melon-flower!

Jenny Kissed Me

LEIGH HUNT

*I found this poem first many years ago and wondered at its
origin. When I first came to London I visited Carlyle's house in
Chelsea and there discovered that Jenny was his wife. The poet
had supposedly written these short lines as a tribute to a lovely
lady.*

Jenny kissed me when we met,
   Jumping from the chair she sat in;
Time, you thief, who love to get
   Sweets into your list, put that in!
Say I'm weary, say I'm sad,
   Say that health and wealth have missed me,
Say I'm growing old, but add –
   Jenny kissed me.

Lake Isle of Innisfree   W. B. YEATS

Growing up in Australia with stories of Scottish relations this poem epitomized what I thought I was missing. I vowed to have a small house where I could grow vegetables, listen to the birds, watch the water and live in peace. I'm still dreaming of my "Innisfree".

I will arise and go now, and go to Innisfree,
    And a small cabin build there, of clay and wattles made:
Nine bean rows will I have there, a hive for the honey bee,
    And live alone in the bee-loud glade.

And I shall have some peace there, for peace comes dropping
      slow
    Dropping from the veils of the morning to where the cricket
      sings;
There midnight's all a-glimmer, and noon a purple glow,
    And evening full of the linnet's wings.

I will arise and go now, for always night and day
    I hear lake water lapping with low sounds by the shore;
While I stand on the roadway, or on the pavements grey,
    I hear it in the deep heart's core.

The Nightingale and the Glow-worm

WILLIAM COWPER

A tiny glow-worm, threatened with being supper for a nightingale, defends his right to life. A parable for all who feel overwhelmed by force and size, this shows the little person can succeed by wit and confidence.

A nightingale that all day long
Had cheered the village with his song,
Nor yet at eve his note suspended,
Nor yet when eventide was ended,
Began to feel, as well he might,
The keen demands of appetite;
When, looking eagerly around,
He spied far off, upon the ground,
A something shining in the dark,
And knew the glow-worm by his spark;
So, stooping down from hawthorn top,
He thought to put him in his crop.

The worm, aware of his intent,
Harangued him thus, right eloquent:
"Did you admire my lamp," quoth he,
"As much as I your minstrelsy,
You would abhor to do me wrong
As much as I to spoil your song:
For 'twas the self-same Power Divine
Taught you to sing and me to shine,
That you with music, I with light,
Might beautify and cheer the night."

The songster heard this short oration.
And, warbling out his approbation,
Released him, as my story tells,
And found a supper somewhere else.

On His Blindness JOHN MILTON

*When I was at school this poem was on a reading list. I liked
the way Milton wrote and as a result bought my first volume of
the collected verse of one poet. There is pride of achievement
in these words and also a humility in handicap. The last line is
one often used by people who have not read what goes before
and therefore only half understand what Milton has said.*

When I consider how my light is spent,
   E're half my days, in this dark world and wide,
   And the one Talent which is death to hide,
   Lodg'd with me useless, though my soul more bent
To serve therewith my maker, and present
   My true account, least he returning chide,
   Doth God exact day-labour, light deny'd,
   I fondly ask; But Patience to prevent
That murmur, soon replies, God doth not need
   Either man's work or his own gifts, who best
   Bear his milde yoke, they serve him best, his state
Is kingly. Thousands at his bidding speed
   And post o're Land and Ocean without rest:
They also serve who only stand and wait.

The Passionate Shepherd to His Love

CHRISTOPHER MARLOWE

*More strange English, with language which now seems archaic.
But there is nothing old in the sentiments expressed here. A
young man offers inducement to his lady. Does she accept?*

Come liue with mee and be my loue,
And we will all the pleasures proue,
That hills and valleys, dales and fields,
And all the craggy mountain yeeldes.

There we will sit vpon the Rocks,
And see the sheepheards feede theyr flocks
By shallow riuers, to whose falls
Melodious byrds sing Madrigalls.

And I will make thee beds of Roses,
And a thousand fragrant poesies,
A cap of flowers, and a kirtle,
Imbroydered all with leaues of Mirtle.

A gowne made of the finest wooll,
Which from our pretty Lambes we pull,
Fayre lined slippers for the cold,
With buckles of the purest gold.

A belt of straw and Iuie buds,
With Corall clasps and Amber studs,
And if these plesures may thee moue,
Come liue with mee, and be my loue.

The Soldier

RUPERT BROOKE

*Brooke did die in a foreign field, but he left these lovely words
telling of his love for England. Perhaps his England is not ours,
but wherever we live there is something in these lines to
remind us of home.*

If I should die, think only this of me:
   That there's some corner of a foreign field
That is for ever England. There shall be
   In that rich earth a richer dust concealed,
A dust which England bore, shaped, made aware,
   Gave, once, her flowers to love, her ways to roam,
A body of England's, breathing English air,
   Washed by the rivers, blest by suns of home.
And think this heart, all evil shed away,
   A pulse in the eternal mind; no less
Gives somewhere back the thoughts by England given;
Her sights and sounds; dreams happy as her day;
   And laughter, learnt of friends; and gentleness,
In hearts at peace, under an English heaven.

My Beloved

THE BIBLE *(Authorized version)*
From *The Song of Solomon* Chapter 5, verses 10–16

This is probably one of the most beautiful passages in the Bible. It is a love song which carefully and emotionally details the attributes of a lover who is also a friend.

10 My beloved is white and ruddy, the chiefest among ten thousand.

11 His head is as the most fine gold, his locks are bushy, and black as a raven.

12 His eyes are as the eyes of doves by the rivers of waters, washed with milk, and fitly set.

13 His cheeks are as a bed of spices, as sweet flowers: his lips like lilies, dropping sweet smelling myrrh.

14 His hands are as gold rings set with the beryl: his belly is as bright ivory overlaid with sapphires.

15 His legs are as pillars of marble, set upon sockets of fine gold: his countenance is as Lebanon, excellent as the cedars.

16 His mouth is most sweet: yea, he is altogether lovely. This is my beloved, and this is my friend, O daughters of Jerusalem.

Sonnet 18

WILLIAM SHAKESPEARE

*Love poems come in many guises. This one waxes lyrical on
the beauty of a woman and is a fitting partner to the Song of
Solomon. Language such as is found in these two poems shows
how expressive English can be when used with skill.*

Shall I compare thee to a summer's day?
Thou art more lovely and more temperate:
Rough winds do shake the darling buds of May,
And summer's lease hath all too short a date:
Sometime too hot the eye of heaven shines,
And often is his gold complexion dimm'd:
And every fair from fair sometime declines,
By chance, or nature's changing course untrimm'd;
But thy eternal summer shall not fade,
Nor lose possession of that fair thou ow'st,
Nor shall death brag thou wander'st in his shade,
When in eternal lines to time thou grow'st;
   So long as men can breathe, or eyes can see,
   So long lives this, and this gives life to thee.

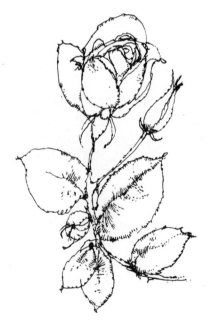

Stupidity Street

RALPH HODGSON

*At first glance these short lines appear ephemeral, but look
again. I found this as a child and was immediately appalled
without truly understanding the full meaning of the poem.
Ecology is a circle, and here it is explained starkly and without
compromise.*

I saw with open eyes
   Singing birds sweet
Sold in the shops
   For the people to eat,
Sold in the shops of
   Stupidity Street.

I saw in a vision
   The worm in the wheat,
And in the shops nothing
   For people to eat;
Nothing for sale in
   Stupidity Street.

To be Sung or Chanted

Battle-Hymn of the Republic

JULIA WARD HOWE

The American Civil War set families fighting each other, yet out of it came hymns and songs such as this. It needs to be sung if you know the tune, but chanting it while walking is a stirring experience. The truth of the words still stands.

Mine eyes have seen the glory of the coming of the Lord:
He is trampling out the vintage where the grapes of wrath are
    stored;
He hath loosed the fateful lightning of His terrible swift sword:
    His truth is marching on.

I have seen Him in the watch-fires of a hundred circling camps;
They have builded Him an altar in the evening dews and damps;
I can read His righteous sentence by the dim and flaring lamps:
    His day is marching on.

I have read a fiery gospel writ in burnished rows of steel:
"As ye deal with my contemners so with you My grace shall deal;
Let the Hero, born of woman, crush the serpent with His heel,
    Since God is marching on."

He hath sounded forth the trumpet that shall never call retreat;
He is sifting out the hearts of men before His judgment-seat:
Oh, be swift, my soul, to answer Him! Be jubilant, my feet!
    Our God is marching on.

In the beauty of the lilies Christ was born across the sea,
With a glory in His bosom that transfigures you and me:
As He died to make men holy, let us die to make men free!
    While God is marching on.

The Bells of London Town

TRADITIONAL

*Most people know a few verses; here is all of the rhyme. If you
have an opportunity, try to visit some of the churches
mentioned. Not many are left. St Clement Danes still plays the
tune each day and still holds an oranges and lemons service
each year.*

Gay go up, and gay go down,
To ring the bells of London town.

Bull's eyes and targets
Say the bells of St. Margaret's.

Brickbats and tiles,
Say the bells of St. Giles.

Halfpence and farthings,
Say the bells of St. Martin's.

Oranges and lemons,
Say the bells of St. Clement's.

Pancakes and fritters,
Say the bells of St. Peter's.

Two sticks and an apple,
Say the bells of Whitechapel.

Old Father Baldpate,
Say the slow bells at Aldgate.

You owe me ten shillings,
Say the bells of St. Helen's.

Pokers and tongs,
Say the bells of St. John's.

Kettles and pans,
Say the bells of St. Anne's.

When will you pay me?
Say the bells of Old Bailey.

When I grow rich,
Say the bells of Shoreditch.

Pray when will that be?
Say the bells at Stepney.

I am sure I don't know,
Says the great bell at Bow.

Here comes a candle to light you to bed,
And here comes a chopper to chop off your head.

The Best School of All

SIR HENRY NEWBOLT

This was my school song and I sang it every day for some years. It's sentimental, patriotic and long. However, despite all that reading, it recalls the memory of a younger me standing in tunic and blazer heartily belting out the words, full of school pride.

It's good to see the school we knew,
    The land of youth and dream,
To greet again the rule we knew
    Before we took the stream:
Though long we've missed the sight of her,
    Our hearts may not forget;
We've lost the old delight of her,
    We keep her honour yet.

We'll honour yet the school we knew,
    The best school of all:
We'll honour yet the rule we knew,
    Till the last bell call.
For, working days or holidays,
And glad or melancholy days,
They were great days and jolly days
    At the best school of all.

The stars and sounding vanities
    That half the crowd bewitch,
What are they but inanities
    To him that treads the pitch?
And where's the wealth, I'm wondering,
    Could buy the cheers that roll
When the last charge goes thundering
    Beneath the twilight goal?

The men that tanned the hide of us,
    Our daily foes and friends,
They shall not lose their pride of us
    Howe'er the journey ends.
Their voice to us who sing of it
    No more its message bears,
But the round world shall ring of it
    And all we are be theirs.

To speak of Fame a venture is,
    There's little here can bide,
But we may face the centuries,
    And dare the deepening tide:
For though the dust that's part of us
    To dust again be gone,
Yet here shall beat the heart of us:
    The school we handed on!

We'll honour yet the school we knew,
    The best school of all:
We'll honour yet the rule we knew,
    Till the last bell call.
For, working days or holidays,
And glad or melancholy days,
They were great days and jolly days
    At the best school of all.

Between Yourself and Me

LEWIS CARROLL

There is a tune to this, but you don't need it, as the words sing themselves. It's nonsense; trying to keep track of who said what is impossible. Just relax and enjoy the sheer fun of the secret.

They told me you had been to her,
   And mentioned me to him:
She gave me a good character,
   But said I could not swim.

He sent them word I had not gone,
   (We know it to be true):
If she should push the matter on,
   What would become of you?

I gave her one, they gave him two,
   You gave us three or more;
They all returned from him to you,
   Though they were mine before.

If I or she should chance to be
   Involved in this affair,
He trusts to you to set them free,
   Exactly as we were.

My notion was that you had been
   (Before she had this fit)
An obstacle that came between
   Him, and ourselves, and it.

Don't let him know she liked them best,
   For this must ever be
A secret, kept from all the rest,
   Between yourself and me.

Drake's Drum   SIR HENRY NEWBOLT

*This is best chanted to an accompaniment of sombre drum
beats. It's a good story, Drake imagined as a supporter and
guardian angel of ships, his drum hanging ready to summon
assistance. Seamen are superstitious, and this poem offers
comfort in times of stress.*

Drake he's in his hammock an' a thousand mile away,
    (Capten, art tha sleepin' there below?),
Slung atween the round shot in Nombre Dios Bay,
    An' dreamin' arl the time o' Plymouth Hoe.
Yarnder lumes the Island, yarnder lie the ships,
    Wi' sailor lads a-dancin' heel-an'-toe,
An' the shore-lights flashin', an' the night-tide dashin',
    He sees et arl so plainly as he saw et long ago.

Drake he was a Devon man, an' rüled the Devon seas,
    (Capten, art tha sleepin' there below?),
Rovin' tho' his death fell, he went wi' heart at ease,
    An' dreamin' arl the time o' Plymouth Hoe.
"Take my drum to England, hang et by the shore,
    Strike et when your powder's runnin' low;
If the Dons sight Devon, I'll quit the port o' Heaven,
    An' drum them up the Channel as we drumm'd them long
      ago."

Drake he's in his hammock till the great Armadas come,
    (Capten, art tha sleepin' there below?),
Slung atween the round shot, listenin' for the drum,
    An' dreamin' arl the time o' Plymouth Hoe.
Call him on the deep sea, call him up the Sound,
    Call him when ye sail to meet the foe;
Where the old trade's plyin' an' the old flag's flyin'
    They shall find him ware an' wakin', as they found him long
      ago!

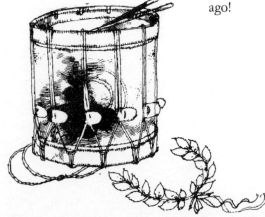

I Hear America Singing

WALT WHITMAN

Patriotic fervour shines through these words as the poet
praises the work of each individual who is part of the whole
which makes America. It could equally be a national statement
for other countries.

I hear America singing, the varied carols I hear,
Those of mechanics, each one singing his as it should be blithe
 and strong,
The carpenter singing his as he measures his plank or beam,
The mason singing his as he makes ready for work, or leaves off
 work,
The boatman singing what belongs to him in his boat, the
 deckhand singing on the steamboat deck,

The shoemaker singing as he sits on his bench, the hatter
 singing as he stands,
The wood-cutter's song, the ploughboy's on his way in the
 morning, or at noon intermission or at sundown,
The delicious singing of the mother, or of the young wife at
 work, or of the girl sewing or washing,
Each singing what belongs to him or her and to none else,
The day what belongs to the day – at night the party of young
 fellows, robust, friendly,
Singing with open mouths their strong melodious songs.

Jerusalem

WILLIAM BLAKE

*I find this very stirring to sing or read. The music surges
through to carry the singer to a climax, while the words allow
reflection without music. Either way this says for England what
Walt Whitman says for America.*

And did those feet in ancient time
   Walk upon England's mountains green
And was the holy Lamb of God
   On England's pleasant pastures seen?

And did the Countenance Divine
   Shine forth upon our clouded hills?
And was Jerusalem builded here
   Among these dark Satanic Mills?

Bring me my bow of burning gold!
   Bring me my arrows of desire!
Bring me my spear: O clouds, unfold!
   Bring me my chariot of fire!

I will not cease from mental fight,
   Nor shall my sword sleep in my hand,
Till we have built Jerusalem
   In England's green and pleasant land.

The Lamb   WILLIAM BLAKE

I don't know of a tune for this poem, but the words seem to sing of their own volition. This is a far more gentle poem than the one about the tiger. The religious imagery gives it a twofold meaning.

Little Lamb, who made thee?
Dost thou know who made thee?
Gave thee life, and bid thee feed,
By the stream and o'er the mead;
Gave thee clothing of delight,
Softest clothing, woolly, bright;
Gave thee such a tender voice,
Making all the vales rejoice?
Little Lamb, who made thee?
Dost thou know who made thee?

Little Lamb, I'll tell thee,
Little Lamb, I'll tell thee:
He is calléd by thy name,
For He calls Himself a Lamb.
He is meek, and He is mild;
He became a little child
I a child, and thou a lamb,
We are calléd by His name.
Little Lamb, God bless thee!
Little Lamb, God bless thee!

Lord Randal

ANONYMOUS

A sad tale this, wrapped in repeated lines so that you need to look hard for the story. A nonchalant rendering of intrigue and suspected murder.

"O where hae ye been, Lord Randal, my son?
O where hae ye been, my handsome young man?"
"I hae been to the wild wood; mother, make my bed soon,
For I'm weary wi' hunting, and fain wald lie down."

"Where gat ye your dinner, Lord Randal, my son?
Where gat ye your dinner, my handsome young man?"
"I din'd wi' my true-love; mother, make my bed soon,
For I'm weary wi' hunting, and fain wald lie down."

"What gat ye to your dinner, Lord Randal, my son?
What gat ye to your dinner, my handsome young man?"
"I gat eels boil'd in broo; mother, make my bed soon,
For I'm weary wi' hunting, and fain wald lie down."

"What became of your bloodhounds, Lord Randal, my son?
What became of your bloodhounds, my handsome young man?"
"O they swell'd and they died; mother, make my bed soon,
For I'm weary wi' hunting, and fain wald lie down."

"O I fear ye are poison'd, Lord Randal, my son!
O I fear ye are poison'd, my handsome young man!"
"O yes! I am poison'd; mother, make my bed soon,
For I'm sick at the heart, and I fain wald lie down."

The Minstrel Boy   THOMAS MOORE

*Ireland has long been a troubled land, its men and women
fighting for freedom of religion, government and life itself. It is
also a land of song, and many Irish warriors are also gifted
musicians. The horror of war for this young man also meant
the end of his singing, for he would not produce music in
captivity.*

The minstrel boy to the war is gone,
   In the ranks of death you'll find him:
His father's sword he has girded on,
   And his wild harp slung behind him.
"Land of song," said the warrior bard,
   "Though all the world betrays thee,
One sword, at least, thy rights shall guard,
   One faithful harp shall praise thee!"

The minstrel fell, but the foeman's chain
   Could not bring his proud soul under;
The harp he loved ne'er spoke again,
   For he tore its chords asunder:
And said:"No chains shall sully thee,
   Thou soul of love and bravery!
Thy songs were made for the brave and free
   They shall never sound in slavery!"

My Country
DOROTHEA McKELLAR

*When I was at school every child knew verse two, and it was
years before I discovered that there was more and that it began
in England. The poet was born in England and emigrated to
Australia at the age of 19. She loved her adopted country so
much that this poem now epitomises for many people the
harsh beauty of the Great South Land.*

The love of field and coppice,
　Of green and shaded lanes,
Of ordered woods and gardens
　Is running in your veins.
Strong love of grey-blue distance
　Brown streams and soft, dim skies –
I know but cannot share it,
　My love is otherwise.

I love a sunburnt country,
　A land of sweeping plains,
Of ragged mountain ranges,
　Of droughts and flooding rains.
I love her far horizons,
　I love her jewel-sea,
Her beauty and her terror –
　The wide brown land for me!

The stark white ring-barked forests,
　All tragic to the moon,
The sapphire-misted mountains,
　The hot gold hush of noon.
Green tangle of the brushes,
　Where lithe lianas coil,
And orchids deck the tree tops
　And ferns the warm dark soil.

Core of my heart, my country!
　　Her pitiless blue sky,
When sick at heart, around us,
　　We see the cattle die –
But then the grey clouds gather,
　　And we can bless again
The drumming of an army,
　　The steady, soaking rain.

Core of my heart, my country!
　　Land of the Rainbow Gold,
For flood and fire and famine,
　　She pays us back three-fold.
Over the thirsty paddocks,
　　Watch, after many days,
The filmy veil of greenness
　　That thickens as we gaze ....

An opal-hearted country,
　　A wilful, lavish land –
All you who have not loved her,
　　You will not understand –
Though earth holds many splendours,
　　Wherever I may die,
I know to what brown country
　　My homing thoughts will fly.

Psalm 121

THE BIBLE (*Authorized version*)
A Song of degrees.

*This is my favourite psalm and I am reminded of it every time
I go to Wales or Scotland, or fly over the mountains of Europe.
The majesty of the peaks is a reminder to me of the
awesomeness of God.*

1 I will lift up mine eyes unto the hills, from whence cometh
my help.

2 My help cometh from the LORD, which made heaven and
earth.

3 He will not suffer thy foot to be moved: he that keepeth
thee will not slumber.

4 Behold, he that keepeth Israel shall neither slumber nor
sleep.

5 The LORD is thy keeper: the LORD is thy shade upon they
right hand.

6 The sun shall not smite thee by day, nor the moon by night.

7 The LORD shall preserve thee from all evil: he shall
preserve thy soul.

8 The LORD shall preserve thy going out and thy coming in
from this time forth, and even for evermore.

A Red, Red Rose ROBERT BURNS

*Burns wrote some fine verse, but much of it is in dialect. This
one is fairly easy to understand if read aloud, better still if sung.
Another love poem, but this time the gentleman is expansive
in his promises, saying he will love until "the seas gang dry".*

O, my luve's like a red, red rose,
   That's newly sprung in June:
O, my luve's like the melodie
   That's sweetly played in tune.

As fair art thou, my bonnie lass,
   So deep in luve am I;
And I will luve thee still, my dear,
   Till a' the seas gang dry.

Till a' the seas gang dry, my dear,
   And the rocks melt wi' the sun:
And I will luve thee still, my dear,
   While the sands o' life shall run.

And fare thee well, my only luve!
   And fare thee well a while!
And I will come again, my luve,
   Though it were ten thousand mile.

The Streets of Laredo ANONYMOUS

*A sad cowboy song. There is pathos in this, regret at a lost life,
and a moral for those left behind.*

As I walked out in the streets of Laredo,
As I walked out in Laredo one day,
I spied a young cowboy all wrapped in white linen
All wrapped in white linen as cold as the clay.

"I see by your outfit that you are a cowboy" –
These words he did say as I boldly stepped by,
"Come sit down beside me and hear my sad story;
I'm shot in the breast and I know I must die.

"It was once in the saddle I used to go dashing,
Once in the saddle I used to go gay;
First to the ale-house and then to the jail-house,
Got shot in the breast and I'm dying today.

"Get six jolly cowboys to carry my coffin;
Get six pretty maidens to carry my pall;
Put bunches of roses all over my coffin,
Roses to deaden the clods as they fall.

"Oh, beat the drum slowly and play the fife lowly,
Play the dead march as you carry me along;
Take me to the green valley and lay the sod o'er me,
For I'm a young cowboy and I know I've done wrong.

"Go gather around you a crowd of young cowboys
And tell them the story of this, my sad fate;
Tell one and the other before they go further
To stop their wild roving before it's too late.

"Go fetch me a cup, a cup of cold water
To cool my parched lips," the cowboy then said.
Before I returned, the spirit had left him
And gone to its Maker – the cowboy was dead.

We beat the drum slowly and played the fife lowly,
And bitterly wept as we carried him along;
For we all loved our comrade, so brave, young and handsome,
We all loved our comrade although he'd done wrong.

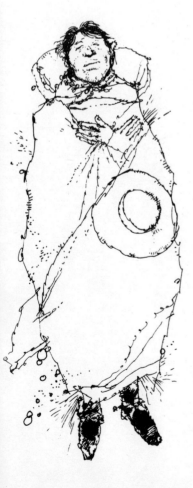

Trees

JOYCE KILMER

*Just a few lines, but they clearly tell of the joy a tree can bring
to those who are prepared to watch and listen. There is a tune
to this, but the words sing by themselves.*

I think that I shall never see
A poem lovely as a tree,
A tree whose hungry mouth is prest
Against the earth's sweet, flowing breast;
A tree that looks at God all day,
And lifts her leafy arms to pray;
A tree that may in summer wear
A nest of robins in her hair;
Upon whose bosom snow has lain;
Who intimately lives with rain.
Poems are made by fools like me.
But only God can make a tree.

Acknowledgements

The compiler and publishers would like to thank the following for permission to include copyright material:

Pam Ayres: "Oh, I Wish I'd Looked After Me Teeth", copyright © Pam Ayres, reprinted by permission of Dolphin Concert Productions Ltd.,

Patrick Barrington: "I Had a Hippopotamus", reprinted by permission of Punch,

Hilaire Belloc: "Tarantella", from *Sonnets and Verses* published by Gerald Duckworth & Co Ltd., reprinted by permission of the Peters Fraser & Dunlop Group Ltd.,

John Betjeman: "Harvest Hymn", from *Collected Poems* by John Betjeman, reprinted by permission of John Murray (Publishers) Ltd.,

Charles Causley: "Colonel Fazackerley", from *Figgie Hobbin* published by Macmillan London, reprinted by permission of David Higham Associates Ltd.,

Walter de la Mare: "The Listeners", reprinted by permission of the Literary Trustees of Walter de la Mare and The Society of Authors as their representative,

Marriott Edgar: "The Lion and Albert", © 1932 Francis, Day & Hunter Ltd., London WC2H 0EA. Reproduced by permission of EMI Music Publishing and International Music Publications,

T. S. Eliot: "The Journey of the Magi", from *Collected Poems 1909–1962* by T. S. Eliot, reprinted by permission of Faber and Faber Ltd.,

Eleanor Farjeon: "Griselda", from *The Children's Bells*, published by Oxford University Press, reprinted by permission of David Higham Associates Ltd.,

Ralph Hodgson: "Stupidity Street", from *Collected Poems* by Ralph Hodgson, reprinted by permission of Mrs Hodgson and Macmillan, London and Basingstoke,

Rex Ingamells: "Platypus and Kookaburra", © Rex Ingamells Estate, 1944, reprinted by permission of Angus & Robertson Publishers/Collins,

Roger McGough: "Who Can Remember Emily Frying?" from *Melting Into the Foreground* published by Viking Kestrel, reprinted by permission of the Peters, Fraser & Dunlop Group Ltd.,

Dorothea McKellar: "My Country", by permission Estate of the late Dorothea Mackellar c/o Curtis Brown (Aust) Pty Ltd.,

Louis MacNeice: "Bagpipe Music", reprinted by permission of Faber and Faber Ltd from *The Collected Poems of Louis MacNeice*,

John Masefield: "Cargoes" and "Sea Fever", reprinted by permission of The Society of Authors as the literary representatives of the Estate of John Masefield,

Rosalie Moore: "Catalogue", reprinted by permission; © 1940, 1968 The New Yorker Magazine, Inc.,

Alfred Noyes: "The Highwayman", from *Collected Poems*, reprinted by permission of John Murray (Publishers) Ltd.,

John O'Brien: "When the Circus Came to Town" by John O'Brien from *Around the Boree Log*, © F. A. Mecham, 1921, reprinted by permission of Angus & Robertson Publishers/Collins,

A. B. Paterson: "A Bush Christening" and "The Man From Snowy River", by A. B. Paterson from *The Collected Verse of A. B. Paterson*, © Retusa Pty. Limited 1921, reprinted by permission of Angus & Robertson Publishers/Collins,

E. V. Rieu: "Sir Smasham Uppe", reprinted by permission of Richard Rieu,

T. Lawrence Selbert: "Casey Jones", © 1912 Shapiro Bernstein & Co. Inc., U.S.A., sub-published Francis, Day & Hunter, London WC2H 0EA, reproduced by permission of EMI Music Publishing and International Music Publications,

Ogden Nash: "The Adventures of Isabel" and "The Tale of Custard the Dragon", © Ogden Nash 1945, reproduced with kind permission of Curtis Brown, London, Iain Crighton Smith: "Robin", reprinted by permission of the author,

Dylan Thomas: "Do Not Go Gentle Into That Good Night", from *The Poems* published by J. M. Dent & Co. Ltd., reprinted by permission of the Trustees for the copyright of Dylan Thomas and David Higham Associates Ltd.,

W. B. Yeats: "The Lake Isle of Innisfree", from *The Collected Poems of W. B. Yeats*, reprinted by permission of A. P. Watt Ltd., on behalf of Michael B. Yeats and Macmillan London Ltd.

While every effort has been made to secure permission, we may have failed in a few cases to trace the copyright holder. We apologise for any apparent negligence.

Index of authors

Index of First Lines